DANCING ON A STAMP

Startling Revelations
From the Other Side

by

Garnet Schulhauser

PO Box 754, Huntsville, AR 72740
www.ozarkmt.com
800-935-0045 or 479-738-2348

For permission, serialization, condensation, adaptions, or for our catalog of other publications, write to Ozark Mountain Publishing, Inc., P.O. box 754, Huntsville, AR 72740, ATTN: Permissions Department.

Library of Congress Cataloging-in-Publication Data
Schulhauser, Garnet, 1951-
   Dancing on a Stamp, by Garnet Schulhauser
A chance meeting with a homeless man marks the beginning of enlightening and soul searching conversations with Garnet's Spirit Guide answering all of the probing questions we all want to know about life here as well as the here after.

1. Spirit Guides   2. Reincarnation   3. Life after Death   4. Religion
I. Schulhauser, Garnet, 1951-   II. Reincarnation   III. Metaphysics
IV. Title

Library of Congress Catalog Card Number: 2012946785

ISBN: 978-1-886940-32-1

Cover Art and Layout: www.enki3d.com
Book set in: Times New Roman
Book Design: Julia Degan

Published by:

OZARK
MOUNTAIN
PUBLISHING

PO Box 754
Huntsville, AR 72740
WWW.OZARKMT.COM
Printed in the United States of America

To Cathy, Blake, Lauren, and Colin.

Acknowledgments

There are many people I want to acknowledge and thank for their contributions toward the writing and publication of *Dancing on a Stamp.* I truly appreciate all the advice, encouragement, and inspiration I received during the course of this endeavor.

First, my thanks to Ozark Mountain Publishing, Inc. for publishing my book and providing me with expert advice and guidance throughout the process and to IteRa Clehouse for her thorough and thoughtful editing of my manuscript.

I would like to acknowledge and thank Ron and Pat Smith for their comments on my manuscript and sage advice on how to maneuver through the enigmatic maze of the publishing world; Ivy Young for her skillful editing and much needed encouragement and advice; Dorothy Ellan for her insight and guidance at crucial times during this project; and our miniature Schnauzer, Abby, who demonstrated over and over the magic of unconditional love.

Special thanks to my sons, Blake and Colin, and my daughter-in-law, Lauren, for all of their love and support.

And last, but most importantly, heartfelt thanks to my wife, Cathy, for her unwavering love, encouragement, advice, and friendship over the years, especially during those times when I was disheartened and in need of a lift.

Table of Contents

Dancing on a Stamp

Introduction

In 2007, my life was mostly on track. I was happily married to a remarkable woman who was a loving and devoted wife and mother. We had two bright and talented sons, both nearing the completion of their college degrees, and we took great pride in watching them mature into adulthood. I had a successful career as a corporate lawyer with a major law firm while my wife cheerfully embraced all the challenges and rewards that arose from her profession as a public health nurse. We lived in a nice house in an upscale neighborhood and enjoyed the material comforts of life that came with financial prosperity. We were happy, healthy, and blessed with many good friends.

Despite all of this good fortune, however, I yearned for something which had eluded me to that point in my life. I wanted the answers to all the big questions about life and death, which all too often roiled my mind, leaving me unsettled and dispirited.

Why am I here? I wondered. *What, if anything, am I supposed to accomplish in my life? Did God select this life for me, or did the Universe assign it by chance? Is all the stuff I learned in Sunday school about God and the afterlife the real truth, or just a lot hooey? Will God judge me when I die and send me to heaven or hell, based on how I lived my life? Does God really exist? Is it possible that when I die I will simply cease to exist—disappearing into nothingness?*

When I recalled my upbringing in a very religious Roman Catholic family, I remembered the answers to these questions that the Catholic Church had taught me when I was a child:

God put me in this life to serve His purpose (which was not apparent to me) and to live my life according the all the rules of the Catholic Church, including those which dictated when, where, and how I was supposed to worship God. When I died, I would appear before God to receive His judgment based on what I did or did not do while on Earth. If I had been good, God would let me enter a wonderful place called heaven where I would enjoy nothing but happiness and bliss for eternity. If I had been bad, God would send me to hell to suffer in its burning fires forever. Or if I had been only semi-bad, I would have to serve time in purgatory until my Soul had been cleansed of my sins, whereupon I would be allowed into heaven.

The Catholic Church's explanation for all this did not sit well with me. Although I had swallowed all of its dogma as a child, I had realized in my twenties that much of what the Church preached to its members did not make any sense when held up to the light and examined with a critical eye. For many years after that, I drifted in no-man's land—not accepting the Catholic Church's dogma but not finding another paradigm to replace it.

At the other end of the spectrum, I knew that many atheists denied the existence of God and believed that we were slotted into our lives on this planet randomly, without any particular purpose, by an impersonal universe. Furthermore, death would be the end for us—we would not continue to exist in an afterlife of any kind. We would simply disappear into the void as our physical bodies returned to dust.

This belief did not feel right to me either although I had no rational explanation for this feeling. My gut reaction was that we all had higher selves or Souls that survived our physical deaths although I wondered sometimes if this was just wishful thinking on my part. Intuitively, I sensed that my life and all other life on this planet was not the result of a series of random events in the universe—that there was a guiding hand of some kind behind it all. I did not subscribe to the Catholic Church's depiction of God as a regal man sitting on a gold throne and dispensing rewards or punishment to the Souls who had finished their lives on Earth. It seemed illogical to me that God, the all-powerful, all-knowing Supreme Being who had everything and lacked nothing, would display many of the negative emotions that are common to humans, such as vanity, jealousy, and anger. *If God had everything,* I wondered, *why did He need to be worshipped by humans in special ways or at all? And why would God give humans free will to live their lives on Earth when it was obvious that this would enable them to breach the rules that He expected them to follow? As well, how do we know that all of "God's rules," dictated to us by the religious holy men who claimed to be speaking for God, actually came from God? Was it possible that these holy men were just following their own personal agendas when they created these rules?*

These questions swirled around in my mind for many years as I searched in vain for the "right" answers that would satisfy my mind and my heart.

Then one sunny afternoon in May of 2007 I took a stroll on a pedestrian mall near my office, and a homeless man stepped out of the shadows and offered to answer all of my vexing questions. I had encountered homeless people on this mall many times before, and I had become quite deft at executing a quick side step to detour around them. But this homeless man was different—his amazing blue eyes penetrated my whole being, right down to the depths of my Soul, and I was riveted to the spot, unable (and unwilling) to move.

This book is based on a series of conversations I had with this homeless man over the next few years. During the course of our discussions, I discovered that this man, whose name was Albert, was not really a homeless person, but was my Spirit Guide in disguise. He told me, much to my surprise, that he and I were old friends who had known each other for a long time although I had no recollection of our previous association. Our conversations were informal, like two friends chatting over a beer, and Albert did his best to give me answers that I could understand and easily communicate to others. Albert had a sharp wit and keen sense of humor, and he was not above using sarcasm to chide me for my many human foibles. My dialogue with Albert was an unforgettable, exhilarating experience, and I am confident, without any doubt, that everything that Albert told me was the "real" truth.

I wrote this book to fulfill Albert's desire that everyone should have the opportunity to read and understand his message to mankind. I find Albert's revelations to be comforting and inspiring and hope you will as well.

Garnet Schulhauser
Vancouver Island
March, 2012

Chapter One

Why Are You Here?

It was another Monday morning. My left eye blinked open as I squinted to read the numbers on the LED clock beside my bed. It was 5:35. I could stay in bed for another hour before I had to get up, so I drifted back into a light sleep as I tried to block out all the thoughts about work that churned through my mind. All I wanted was a few more minutes of sleep.

My left eye blinked open again, with the clock now showing 6:20 in bright red numerals. I slowly swung my legs onto the carpet, trying not to disturb my wife who was sound asleep beside me. Our little dog, Abby, who had slept all night pressed against my leg, gave a quiet sigh and shifted position. I padded silently into the bathroom, clicked on the light, and splashed water on my face to wake up.

Lately, life was making me tired. Although I had everything I had ever hoped for—a devoted wife to love, two wonderful sons, a successful career as a corporate lawyer with a major law firm, and financial prosperity—something was missing. I reached for my electric shaver in the vanity cabinet and plugged it in. I stared into the mirror, and my image stared back at me.

I silently asked myself the same questions I had been asking for years: *Why am I here? Did God select this life for me, or did the universe assign it by chance? When I die, will I go to heaven or hell, or will I merely cease to exist—disappearing into nothingness? Is all that stuff I learned in Sunday school the real truth or just a lot of hooey?* I grappled with these questions as I rubbed the shaver over my face, wondering if I would ever find the answers.

As I ambled into my office that morning, I gave my usual terse "Good Morning" to my assistant as I passed by her desk. I turned on my computer and slowly unloaded my briefcase. I glanced at the tombstone plaques hanging on the wall, each one announcing the completion of a large merger or financing I had done for one of my clients. These successes, which were exciting and rewarding at the time, now felt hollow.

Later that day while still mulling over these questions, I went for a walk on the mall outside our building. It was a warm, sunny afternoon in May, and I breathed deeply as I strolled down the street, weaving my way through the crowd of pedestrians. Suddenly, a street person got up from a bench and stepped in front of me. His clothes were ragged and dirty, his beard was long and unkempt, and his long hair was greasy and stringy. He gave me a gap-toothed smile and looked intently into my eyes.

His bright blue eyes sparkled in the sunlight, and his gaze seemed to penetrate into the depths of my Soul. I sensed that he knew everything about me—my hopes and aspirations, my fears and anxieties, and even the deepest secrets I had never shared with anyone. I started to back away, but I paused because his eyes shone with an unconditional love that permeated my whole body. I stood there unable to move, basking in the soothing warmth that emanated from this man.

The homeless man widened his smile and said, "Why are you here?"

This broke my reverie, but before I had a chance to respond, he turned and slipped into the doorway of a nearby store. I stood there for a few more minutes trying to understand what had happened. *Who was this guy, and why did he stop me on the street? Why did he ask me that question?* I wondered.

I knew I had to catch up to him to find these answers. I entered the store he had ducked into and searched up and down the aisles without any luck. Hoping to spot him, I walked up and down the mall, but he had vanished. I kicked myself for losing sight of this man, and I vowed to return to the mall the next day to see if I could find him.

As I made my way back to my office, more questions swirled in my head. *Where did this homeless man come from, and how did he manage to disappear so quickly?*

That night as I lay in bed, I reflected on the events of the afternoon. I began to think he was not a typical street person, and I had not bumped into him by accident. I recalled a quote I heard years ago which now seemed appropriate: "When the student is ready, the teacher will appear." *Was this homeless man my teacher—or just another bum on the street?*

The next afternoon I went back to the mall, following the same route as the day before. This time I was more alert, glancing back and forth as I searched for the homeless man. After walking for a few blocks and beginning to lose hope, I noticed him sitting alone on a bench. He smiled as his sparkling blue eyes once again infused my whole body with a feeling of love and peace. I felt that nothing could harm me, and I was free from all worldly concerns.

The spell was broken when he spoke, "You have been asking many questions. What would you like to know first?"

[Throughout the dialogue that follows, my words will be in *italics* while Albert's will be in **bold** face.]

Who are you?

> **My name is Albert. I came here to help you.**

How can you help me when you cannot even help yourself? You look like you have been living on the street for weeks, and you smell like a dead fish. What do want from me?

> **Appearances can be deceiving. In your case, you look like a successful lawyer who has everything under control, but underneath that façade, you are really struggling to find meaning in your life.**

How do you know so much about me? I have never seen you before, and I do not know anything about you.

> **We have known each other for a very long time although you do not remember our past. If you would like to find out more, have a seat and I will answer your questions.**

Why should I believe anything you say? For all I know, you are just trying to panhandle money from me.

You cannot be sure at this stage, but what do you have to lose? You can go back to your office to see if you can find your answers in all those emails waiting for you, or you can try your luck with me.

My brain tells me to turn tail and run, but my gut is telling me to stay. I think I will give it a try, so why don't we go back to square one? Who are you and how are you going to help me?

I am a Soul just like you. I am here to answer your questions and guide you on your journey.

What journey?

The journey of your Soul in your current life on Earth.

Why am I on this journey? Did God choose this life for me?

Like all other Souls having a physical incarnation on Earth, you came here to experience what Earth has to offer so you can grow and evolve. The decision to incarnate into the life you now have was made solely by you—it was not dictated by the Creator or anyone else. You chose your life before you were born so you could experience the things necessary for your evolution as a Soul. The Creator did not prepare your script, and It does not manipulate the events in your life.

Who is the Creator? Do you mean God?

The Creator is the totality of everything in the universe. It is the Originator and the essence of everything that exists. Humans have referred to the Creator by many different names with God being the most popular choice. I will follow this common convention by referring to the Creator as God and giving Him a male gender, even though the Creator is neither male nor female.

God created Earth, all the stars and planets, and everything else in the universe. In order to experience all facets of the universe from different perspectives, He also created Souls as individual aspects of Himself that would fan out over the galaxies to experience life wherever it exists in the universe, including Earth. Everything that happens in the universe, including everything experienced by Souls, is experienced by God since all things in the universe are connected to God and to each other, and all are part of the totality that is God. Since all Souls have the free will to choose what they want to experience, each Soul follows its own path for evolution, and this allows God to experience what He has created many different ways.

What does God want me to accomplish in this life?

God does not need you to accomplish anything in your life. He has given you free will to choose your life and plan your journey on Earth. He does not make rules for you to follow, and He will not punish you for anything you do in your life.

Where did I come from before this life?

You came from the Spirit Side, where all Souls come from. You will return to the Spirit Side when you die and leave your body behind. The Spirit Side is all around you although it exists at a higher vibration level than the Earth plane and cannot normally be felt or observed by humans. The Spirit Side is a beautiful place full of love and happiness and is without any disease, pain, or crime. Everyone lives in peace and harmony.

The Spirit Side must be a wonderful place. Is it the same as heaven? Why would anyone want to leave there and come to Earth?

The Spirit Side is, indeed, a wonderful place, much like the heaven described by various religions. You came here knowing that you would be away from the Spirit Side for only a short time, and you would return there when your life as a human had ended. You have done this frequently in the past.

Souls do not consider life on your planet to be a hardship; they view it as an adventure that can provide many rewarding experiences. It is like people who sign up for a two-year job stint in another country. Even though they do not want to leave their homes and move permanently to the new country, they accept this assignment because they expect to enjoy their new adventures in the other country before returning home. They leave with a sense of adventure, knowing that they will learn much about the language and customs of the new country, and this will expand their knowledge and give them a deeper understanding of the world they live in. And even if the new country is not as pleasant as they had hoped, they know they will not be there forever.

Why am I not able to remember anything about the Spirit Side? My life would be so much easier if I could remember the Spirit Side, and I knew with certainty that I will return there when I die.

As part of the incarnation process, you are restricted from directly accessing your memories of the Spirit Side during your life on Earth. A major component of your incarnation is dealing with the unknowns and uncertainties that arise during the course of your life as you seek the answers to your questions about why you are on this journey and what happens when you die.

From my perspective, life is no picnic and many people would agree with a bumper sticker I saw years ago that read: "Life's a bitch. And then you die." Since the Spirit Side is such a happy place and Earth is so difficult, why do Souls seek to endure life on Earth? What can be gained from such a life?

Your question has a complex answer that is not easy for humans to understand. Souls are eternal spirits that seek new experiences by incarnating on Earth in order to learn, gain wisdom, and evolve. Souls on the Spirit Side can learn and acquire knowledge; however, they are not satisfied with knowledge alone. Knowledge with the insight gained through experience becomes wisdom. Souls incarnate into physical bodies to complete their knowledge with experience.

I do not quite follow what you said about knowledge. If I have knowledge on the Spirit Side, why is it important for me to experience things as a human?

Although you do not understand this concept now, it was easy for you to grasp when you were on the Spirit Side. A simple analogy might be helpful. Imagine that you are a child living in a small village in Kenya, and you have never traveled very far from your home and its equatorial climate. If you were in school and studying weather, you would learn that the air temperature in parts of the Northern Hemisphere would often drop down to -20 during the winter months, which could result in frostbite or death to an unprotected human body. Even with all this knowledge about sub-zero temperatures, however, you would still not fully appreciate such cold and its effect on a human body. Your knowledge would not be complete, and you would not have a full understanding of these temperatures unless you traveled to Alaska or Siberia in the middle of January and stood outside with nothing on. This exposure would complete your knowledge of the cold.

Likewise with other physical conditions encountered on Earth, including wind, rain, hunger, disease, and pain, or the negative emotions that are common to humans, such as fear, anger, and hatred. None of these physical attributes or negative emotions exist on the

Spirit Side. You must incarnate in a physical body to experience them.

Why would a Soul want to experience hatred or pain?

All Souls are eager to learn more about themselves and the universe so that they can evolve and grow. Earth has a diversity of physical conditions and negative emotions that Souls desire to experience to advance their evolution. These harsh conditions provide Souls the opportunity to appreciate more fully the unconditional love and happiness they enjoy on the Spirit Side. Souls view a life on Earth as a way of testing themselves to determine if they can endure the pain and hardships they may face without bailing out early and without letting their negative emotions control their actions.

You mentioned that Souls freely choose to incarnate and no one, including God, can dictate that decision. Once a Soul makes the decision to incarnate, who determines where it will be born or the other circumstances of its life?

Souls incarnating into humans are not slotted into bodies by God or by some random act of the universe. Before its incarnation, every Soul creates a Life Plan that is a broad outline of its proposed life. It is designed to provide the Soul with opportunities to encounter the many facets of its planet in order to learn and gain wisdom. The Wise Ones, who are very advanced Souls, review every Life Plan to ensure it is not too difficult or ambitious and that it is appropriate for the Soul. As well, all Life Plans are reviewed by the

10

other Souls who will play significant roles in the Soul's new life. Souls will carefully consider these comments, but ultimately each Soul has the final say in what goes into its Life Plan.

This process would be considered heresy by all the religions that believe God alone decides who we will become and what will happen in our lives. Why would God allow me to create my own Life Plan? What if I create the wrong Life Plan?

There is no such thing as a wrong Life Plan. All Life Plans are equally valid, and God does not make judgments about anyone's Life Plan. God has no interest in controlling the events in anyone's life. God wants every Soul to evolve and grow through the wisdom gained from its journey on Earth, and He is content to allow each Soul to craft its own Life Plan. Just as there is no wrong Life Plan, there is no perfect Life Plan either. If a Life Plan does not create the best opportunities for a Soul to undergo the things it is seeking, there will be other lives and other chances. Souls can incarnate as often as they like. If a Soul does not "get it" in one life, it can come back again and again until it has encountered everything it seeks.

This goes against the conventional belief of most people that "you only go around once, so make the best of it." I have heard this expression hundreds of times. It is a concept taught by many religions. Why do you think they have adopted this belief?

With most religions it is all about control. Their religious leaders want their followers to stay within the fold and follow their rules—many of which deal with when, where, and how their members must worship. These religions believe there must be sanctions and rewards in order to encourage their members to obey their rules, and the carrot and stick approach is often used. If individuals are good during their lives and follow the rules of the religion, they will go to a wonderful place called heaven when they die. On the other hand, if they misbehave and do not follow the rules, they will go to an awful place called hell where they will suffer forever. In order to make the carrot and stick more effective, they decided that each person will have only one chance. What individuals do or do not do in their current lives will determine where they will go when they die. There would be no second chances.

If reincarnation was an option, and people could continue with their lives until they got it right, there would be less urgency to be good in any particular life. People would then be more inclined to follow their earthly desires and not worry about their behavior if they knew they could come back as often as they liked. Without the immediate prospect of going to hell, a person might follow the easy road and ignore the religion's rules until another life. It is like how you might decide to watch a football game on television instead of raking the leaves in your back yard. You know the leaves will still be there tomorrow, so why not enjoy yourself today?

I take your point. These religions would lose much of their clout if their members knew they were not limited to one life. Armed with this knowledge, it would be easier for me to justify skipping church on Sunday so I could spend the day fishing. Moreover, if I happened to die before I had a chance to make amends, I would not be banished to hell forever, and I could come back to Earth in another life and try again.

This is why many religions reject the concept of reincarnation. They believe the best way to keep their followers on the right path is to "hold their feet to the fire" by preaching that they have only one life and one chance to be good (which means following the rules of the religion). Failing to do so, they will be sent to hell to suffer in pain forever.

So it was my decision to incarnate, and I prepared a Life Plan for my life before I was born. Does this mean that everything I do and everything that happens to me is predetermined?

No, everything in your life is not predetermined. Your Life Plan is a broad outline of your life that is subject to change as a result of the decisions you make and your reaction to events. You have the right to exercise your free will on Earth, and this affects how you live within the broad blueprint of your Life Plan. When you are on the Spirit Side, you cannot accurately predict how you as an incarnate Soul will exercise your free will through your conscious decisions and actions. Every Life Plan contains several forks in the road, and you get to choose the path you take at each junction. Every choice you make will have an impact

13

on the rest of your life, and some decisions may cause you to stray a long way off your intended path.

If I know on the Spirit Side what I want to experience in this incarnation, why can't my Soul communicate its intentions to me so I can make the right choices and go down the right path?

There is no absolute right or wrong path for Souls to take. Your Soul *does* try to steer you in the "right" direction (being the direction that is most consistent with your Life Plan), but your conscious mind does not always hear the message or dismisses it through rationalization. Often when you receive an intuitive thought or hear an inner voice directing you to do something, you analyze and rationalize the message and end up ignoring it. Other times you do not hear the message because of all the thoughts that clutter your mind. These messages from your Soul (and from your Spirit Guides) provide you with guidance at important decision points in your life. They do not attempt to give you a detailed picture of your Life Plan, since that would detract from your purpose in being here in the first place.

Let me give you an example that might help you understand. Imagine you are the owner of a small business, and you hear there has been a problem with theft in the shop. You decide to set up a sting to find the thief, so you leave a wallet on a table in a small room off the warehouse and hide a video camera to record the events. Then you arrange for each employee to enter this room alone and unobserved.

14

The video camera will record how each employee reacts to the wallet; most will pick it up and turn it in to you, but a few will take the money for themselves. It is your hope that this set-up will show the true character of each employee and reveal the identity of the culprit. Now run this same scenario again, only this time you tell your employees you have hidden a camera in the room to record what happens.

That would make no sense, since every employee would give the wallet to you without taking the money.

Exactly, and the purpose for the sting would be defeated. Likewise, if you consciously know what is in your Life Plan and what your Soul hopes you will do in each situation, you will make decisions and take actions only in accordance with your Life Plan, even if your inclination was to do otherwise.

If I can change the direction I take by exercising my free will, does this not defeat the whole purpose of having a Life Plan?

Your actions can affect your life in various ways; however, your Life Plan will still be valid as a broad outline of your life. There are several things in your Life Plan that you cannot alter by your free-will decisions, such as the persons who are your parents and siblings, the place you were born, and your physical characteristics. At all important forks in the road, you will be coached to choose the right path (which is the path proposed in your Life Plan). Sometimes "road signs" will guide you, but even if you still miss the intended route, there will be other forks

in the road later in life that will allow you to get back on track.

Who does the coaching and what are the road signs?

The coaching comes from your Spirit Guides. The road signs are occurrences or events in your life designed to steer you down the right path. In most cases, you included the road signs in your Life Plan before you were born although sometimes your Spirit Guides create them after you have begun your life.

Spirit Guides are Souls on the Spirit Side who serve as your coaches while you are on Earth. Every person has several Spirit Guides. Most Spirit Guides have incarnated on Earth themselves, and they can appreciate the difficulties you might encounter during your life. I am one of your Spirit Guides.

I have more questions about Spirit Guides and road signs, but first I would like to understand more about my Life Plan. If I heard you correctly, when I created my Life Plan, I chose my birthplace, my parents and siblings, and my physical characteristics.

That is right.

So when I stare at my mug in the mirror and wonder why I am here in this particular body, the answer is that I chose all of these factors before I was born. If this is true, why did I pick this life? Why did I not choose to be born as someone with a soft and cushy life, like Prince Charles? I read an article on the Internet recently that described his pampered life—he has 150 household servants to look after him, including one who squeezes toothpaste onto to his toothbrush whenever he brushes his teeth.

When you were planning your current incarnation, you were leaning in that direction, but we managed to persuade you that squeezing a tube of toothpaste was an experience you had to have. How a person squeezes the tube can reveal much about his character—some people will squeeze a new tube randomly while others will methodically squeeze from the very bottom and work their way to the top.

Methinks you jest, Albert. But since I have already squeezed countless tubes of toothpaste in my life, can you guys now arrange for someone else to do this for me?

It cannot be done. There is only one person on your planet with the proper tube-squeezing technique, and he works for Prince Charles.

I am glad to know that my Spirit Guides have a sense of humor, no matter how weird it may be.

Humor is alive and well on the Spirit Side. We laugh a lot over here, especially when watching the antics of humans on your planet. Many of your capers have been hilarious even though you were not trying to be funny. I will show you what I mean when you return to the Spirit Side.

I will have to take your word for it. For now, can we get back on track? Can you tell me why I chose the life I have?

Souls choose their lives and develop their Life Plans in order to evolve and grow or to help another Soul encounter the things it needs for its evolution. Often it is a combination of the two. From your Earthly perspective, you think that having a comfortable incarnation with few challenges or hardships would be the best life for you and the easiest one to endure. Although this goal is valid to you now, it did not have any relevance to you on the Spirit Side when you devised your Life Plan. You did not come to Earth to have an easy and trouble-free life since most of the things you had hoped to experience arise from the difficulties and hardships you have faced (and will continue to face) in your life on Earth. You could have planned a soft life, but such a life would not have included all the things you had hoped for during this incarnation. It is not wrong, however, to be well-off and enjoy the comforts of life. In some cases, a Soul will choose a privileged life in order to understand the unique challenges that arise in a life filled with wealth and success. In other situations, wealth or success (or a lack thereof) will not have a significant impact one way or the other on the events a Soul wants to endure, and it will be indifferent as to whether or not they are present during its incarnation.

Are you saying I deliberately planned all the circumstances in my current life, including all the obstacles and negative events that I have lived with so far?

You did plan most of these events although sometimes they arose when you and other people in your life made free-will decisions. When people undergo hardships, they often wonder what they did to deserve such treatment. They will ask God why He is causing them pain and suffering and will frequently become very angry with God for being so cruel. This leads to self-pity when they conclude they had done nothing wrong and life is unfair. Once you acknowledge that you are the author of your reality, you will never again suffer from the victim mentality. Your reality arises from the Life Plan you created for yourself on the Spirit Side and from your reaction to the events that happen to you in this life.

This reminds me of a tale I heard years ago about identical twin boys who were separated at birth. Although they never saw each other again, they lived parallel lives with similar jobs, families, and life events. One of the twins was an optimist by nature and the other was a pessimist. Even though their lives were very similar, the optimist enjoyed a much happier life than the pessimist did because he reacted to the events in his life with a positive attitude while the pessimist reacted in a negative way.

This story makes a good point. Your Life Plan sets out a broad outline of the events to occur in your life, but your free will determines how you react to such events. For example, if a Life Plan contemplates that a

man will be fired from his job when he is thirty-four, his reaction to that event is not predetermined. He might become bitter and depressed, wallowing in self-pity as a victim who has been dealt a cruel blow by God, or he might choose to have a positive attitude, vowing to learn from this setback as he searches for his next job. His Life Plan cannot dictate how he will react to this event—his free-will choices determine his reaction to this event, which affects the reality that follows. If a person responds in a positive way to the obstacles and challenges he lives through, he will enjoy a happier life than if he reacts in a negative manner to these events. It is much better to see the glass as half full than half empty, but that is a choice freely made by each person. You can choose to be happy and fulfilled or unhappy and miserable—it is up to you.

I would like to understand more about Life Plans and how I can alter my course with my free-will actions, but I need time to digest what you have told me so far. Can we resume this discussion at a later time?

Yes, of course. I am always available. Let me know when you want to continue.

Will you do me a favor and take a bath before we meet the next time?

I can do that, as long as you don't wear that tie again.

What is wrong with my tie?

It's a little too bright. If you were stranded on a deserted island in the Pacific, you could wave your tie in the air, and they would see you from space. But here it seems out of place—it just doesn't go with your stuffed shirt.

I think we have a deal. So long for now.

I rose from the bench and waved goodbye to Albert. Feeling both bewildered and elated, I walked back to my office. That night I wrote down everything Albert had said to me as I tried to make sense of my encounter with him. I had just spent part of the afternoon talking to a disheveled street person, a man I would normally ignore. But my intuition told me there was something special about Albert, and I knew I had to continue our conversation.

Chapter Two

Life Plans and Free Will

After my first afternoon on the bench with Albert, I had many more conversations with my Spirit Guide. For the first couple of meetings, Albert appeared to me as the homeless man, but in later sessions Albert spoke to me without appearing in a physical form. (I realized later that I was the only one who could see and hear Albert as the homeless man). Albert always spoke to me by thought transfer or telepathy, and I took notes as best I could. He usually waited for me to begin a session when I was ready, and he has never failed to be available when I have questions.

Out of fear of being committed to a rubber room somewhere, I did not tell anyone, including my wife, about my conversations with Albert. After my first meeting with Albert, my outlook on life changed drastically in light of his assertion that my Soul had selected most of the significant factors in my life before I was born. When I stared at my image in the mirror every morning, I no longer wondered how I got here. Instead, I wanted to understand what I was supposed to do with the rest of my life.

I remembered reading a quote from Yogi Berra: "When you come to a fork in the road, you've got to take it." I hoped someone would help me navigate my next fork.

After reflecting on what Albert had revealed to me, I had more questions for him.

Albert, I would like to know more about Life Plans. You mentioned that when we prepare our Life Plans on the Spirit Side, we do so in conjunction with other Souls. Can you explain how this works?

All lives have connections with other people. When you developed your Life Plan, you coordinated various aspects of your Life Plan with the Souls you planned to interact with in your life. Your Life Plan included particulars of your parents, siblings, relatives, friends, and co-workers. These other Souls agreed beforehand to be part of your life, and you agreed to be part of theirs. This was essential since you could not foist yourself upon someone else's life to any significant degree without their concurrence. They had an opportunity to review your Life Plan and make suggestions (especially about the parts of your Life Plan that involved them), and you did the same with their Life Plans.

How does one go about picking these Souls on the Spirit Side? Do they have a choice, or can I commandeer anyone I want for a particular life?

All Souls belong to one or more spirit groups on the Spirit Side, and most often the significant people in your life are part of your spirit group. Every spirit group consists of Souls who have lived together on Earth before in different relationships. The Soul who was your father in one life may have been your brother or daughter in other lives. Your best friend in this life may have been your spouse or your grandfather in previous lives.

24

Most Souls want to experience Earth to the greatest extent possible, so they will incarnate as both sexes and in a multitude of roles. They will choose to be born in dozens of countries with varied occupations and stations in life. Their physical bodies will vary greatly; sometimes they will be beautiful and athletic, and other times their bodies will be weak or crippled. In some incarnations, they will be poor while in others they will be rich and privileged. Every Soul makes these choices freely when it develops its Life Plan, but it does need the co-operation of other Souls in its spirit group to fill the roles of the people it will interact with in its next life.

What if a Soul cannot find enough volunteers to fill all the roles in its Life Plan?

This does not ever happen. Spirit groups are large enough that a Soul can always find someone to fill all the roles. There is always a feeling of co-operation and goodwill among Souls who understand that if you help another Soul fill a spot in its Life Plan, it will likely return the favor one day.

Imagine that you are the director of a theatrical play. If you have an unattractive part to fill, you may have to call on an actor who owes you a favor from previous plays. Given that the engagement will be relatively short and the fact that an actor can always learn something from every role, you will always be able to find a person to fill the slot. Similarly, Souls on the Spirit Side know that every life is short (relative to

the Spirit Side), so it is not a hardship for a Soul to take on a life primarily to help another Soul.

I am still puzzled about how Life Plans work in relation to the exercise of free will by humans. I understand that when my Soul incarnated, it hoped I would follow the Life Plan it had established for me on the Spirit Side. Since I do not know what is in my Life Plan and I have the ability to make choices, it seems unlikely I will be able to follow my Life Plan very closely. Not only will I stray off course when I make my own free-will decisions, but the actions of other people could also push me down the wrong path. How are these conflicts managed so I can follow my Life Plan?

First of all, you should understand that your Life Plan is only a broad outline of your life; it covers only the major points in your life—it does not fill in all of the details. Most of the everyday things that happen to you do not have a large impact on the important events in your Life Plan. Your free-will actions in response to these matters will not usually cause a serious deviation from your Life Plan although it can happen. Likewise, you will not often stray very far from your course when you interact with other people who are exercising their free will.

As I mentioned before, some of the crucial factors in your Life Plan were in place before you were born, like your place of birth and the people who would be your parents and siblings. Your physical characteristics were determined at conception, including your gender, the color of your skin, and the presence (or lack of) athletic, artistic, and/or other

talent. The country of your birth determined your first language and the customs of your early years. The location of your family's home influenced the choice of schools you attended. The occupations and social status of your parents played an important role in your early development. All of these features were there when you were born, and you could not change them.

What about the things I can change? How can I now prevent a radical departure from my Life Plan when I exercise my free will and when others around me do so as well? When I look back on my life, I can see there were a number of significant occurrences that shaped the rest of my life. For most of these events I was at a fork in the road, and I had to decide which way to go. Since I was not aware of what was in my Life Plan, how did I know which route was best for me? How do I know now that I did take the right path? Is it possible I went the wrong way at a few of those junctures?

You must remember there is no absolute right path to follow on Earth. The path contemplated in your Life Plan is the best path for you to take, but even if you take a wrong path, no one will punish you for doing so, and you will still gain wisdom from your adventures. Nothing that you experience is wasted time; you can still learn much from every life even if you have missed several of the things you need for your evolution. You can have as many lives on Earth as you want, and you can keep coming back until you have done everything you need to do or until additional lives are no longer necessary for your growth as a Soul.

27

There are several things, however, that will guide you to take the right path that will allow you to encounter the main events in your Life Plan. When you created your Life Plan, you inserted a number of "road signs" in strategic places to influence your decisions. When it is necessary, your Spirit Guides will arrange for additional road signs to guide you in the right direction. These road signs can be events that happen in your city or elsewhere in the world, "coincidences" that occur in your life, or things other people say or do. They are designed to steer you on the right path so you can fulfill your Life Plan.

As an example, imagine you have decided to move to another city, and you are searching for a house to buy in the new city. As you struggle to choose between the two houses on your short list, you happen to pick up the local newspaper and notice an article about the terrible traffic snarls that persist in one of the suburbs on your list. With this in mind, you decide to buy the other house. This is not be a coincidence; it is a road sign intended to encourage you to purchase the right house so you can fulfill the agenda set out in your Life Plan.

This reminds me of a series of events that happened to me years ago that had a huge impact on my career. When I was still in law school, a fellow student persuaded me to apply for an articling position in another city, rather than staying close to home. I sent numerous letters of application to law firms in that city, and I lined up a few interviews. After I had finished my last interview, I had a couple of hours to kill before returning home, so I thought I should try to arrange one more interview. I found a phone booth and scanned the yellow pages. My eyes settled on a firm listed under the "B's" and I noted the address. I promptly walked to their office, marched up to the receptionist, and announced that I was there to apply for an articling position. The receptionist called the partner in charge of hiring students. Eventually he appeared and escorted me back to his office. He told me his firm had already hired all the articling students they needed for that year, but the partners had recently decided to hire one more student. The interview went well, and a week later I received an offer from them, which I accepted. I eventually became a partner at this firm, and I practiced law with them for the first fourteen years of my career.

Whenever I have looked back on these events, I always thought I was very lucky I happened to pick this firm out of the yellow pages and have an interview with them without a prior appointment. Fortunately for me, this firm had decided (only days before I had arrived) that they needed one more student. I am still amazed at this remarkable series of coincidences.

There was no luck or chance involved with these events. These "coincidences" were road signs intended to ensure you would end up at the right firm. In fact, there are no coincidences, as such, on Earth. All events that appear to be fortunate occurrences have been arranged deliberately to steer people down the right path.

Frequently when you come to an important fork in the road, you will receive guidance from your Soul and your Spirit Guides on the path you should follow. It might be in the form of an intuitive thought that

suddenly pops into your head, a strong gut feeling, or a message in a dream. Although these messages do not always work, they usually manage to coax you to choose the road that is best suited for you.

On occasion, more dramatic action is required. If your free-will actions (or the actions of other people) would lead to a significant deviation from your intended course, physical intervention from the Spirit Side may be necessary. If a Life Plan provided for a man to live to be eighty-four, and his free-will decisions would cause him to die in a car accident when he was twenty-two, he might be saved from this premature exit by a discreet manipulation of events in his life. For example, the timing sequence of the traffic lights in an intersection might be temporarily altered so he must wait an extra four seconds at the red light, which ensures he will not be entering the next intersection at the same time as another vehicle running the red light, thereby avoiding a deadly crash.

These physical interventions are usually carried out by special spirits on the Spirit Side. Many people believe they have escaped serious injury or death by something that seems like "divine intervention."

Are these special spirits the same as guardian angels? Some religions believe we all have guardian angels to watch over us and protect us from harm. Can you tell me more about the role of these special spirits?

People often call these special spirits guardian angels, and I will use that term for the sake of convenience.

All people have at least one guardian angel to help **them stick** to their Life Plans while they are living on **Earth. Often** these guardian angels send messages in **the form of** intuitive thoughts designed to help people **avoid fatal** accidents not intended in their Life Plans. **When necessary,** they intervene by physically **manipulating events.**

I recall an event from my childhood where divine intervention saved the day. A young couple in our parish had given birth to triplets, who were all somewhat mischievous. One night when they were almost two, their father heard a noise coming from the kitchen, so he got out of bed and walked down the dark hallway toward the noise. When he turned on the light, he found the triplets (who had managed to crawl out of their cribs) running circles around the kitchen table, brandishing large kitchen knives they had found in a drawer. To his amazement (and relief), none of them suffered even a minor scratch. Did their guardian angels protect them from harm?

Most certainly.

But if guardian angels can physically intervene in our lives, does this confirm the widely held belief that God determines what happens in our lives, and we do not have any say or control? This leads us back to fatalism.

Guardian angels do not dictate or control everything that happens to you, they only intervene when it is necessary to enable you to continue with your Life Plan. As I said before, you and everyone else enjoy the freedom of choice, and sometimes these decisions will steer you down a path that is very different from what

you intended in your Life Plan. Guardian angels will intervene to prevent this, as needed. They do not determine everything that happens to you, and they always strive to ensure their interventions do not cause a significant disruption to the lives of the people around you. In my example of the timing changes for the traffic lights, the other vehicles at the first intersection would also have to wait the extra four seconds, but this delay would not have any noticeable impact on the lives of the people in those vehicles.

If guardian angels are there to protect us, why do people die in car crashes?

If a woman dies in a car accident, it is because her Soul decided it was time to depart this life and return to the Spirit Side. That individual's guardian angels allowed the accident to happen to fulfill this desire.

Are you saying our Souls choose when we die?

That is right. No one on Earth dies by accident. You will die when your Soul decides it is time to go even though your mind will not be aware of this decision. Your Life Plan has several built in "exit ramps" that are often changed by your Soul during the course of your life. Your Soul will choose its exit point after carefully considering what it has already experienced and what else remains in its Life Plan. This decision will be made only by your Soul because your mind is not aware of your Soul's agenda, and it will always be inclined to live as long as possible.

I find this hard to accept. Almost every day I read about people dying in car crashes, drive-by shootings, or in explosions detonated by suicide bombers. Several of my relatives and friends have died from heart attacks or terminal cancer. I have difficulty believing that all of these people died because their Souls decided to exit their lives. Often, the people who die tragically at a young age leave behind young children who will have to struggle through the rest of their lives without the love and support of their mom or dad. A Soul's decision to exit does not just affect the person who dies—most often it inflicts hardships on others who had close ties to the deceased person. This seems unfair to all the people who suffer because of this death.

A Soul's decision to exit a human life is not a simple or easy choice to make because everyone on your planet has connections with other people who will be affected by this decision. Even though the people left behind will be surprised and anguished by the death of their loved one, their Souls will understand the process. In many situations, the exit point would have been established beforehand in the person's Life Plan, and all the other Souls would have contemplated this eventuality in their own Life Plans. Although it might appear to be unfair for a two-year-old little girl to lose her mother, the Soul of that child knew about this possibility before it incarnated, and it created its Life Plan with this in mind.

How does my Soul know when I should die? What factors come into play for my Soul to decide which exit point to take?

Every night when you sleep, your Soul leaves your body and goes to the Spirit Side to reflect on your progress to date and consult with your Spirit Guides. Your Soul may choose an earlier departure if your life is especially difficult, and you need to bail out as soon as possible, or your Soul may conclude that it has already passed most of the milestones in its Life Plan and continuing the current life would not be very fruitful. Your Soul will evaluate its progress on a continual basis and then choose the exit point that best suits its needs.

What happens if my Soul decides on an early exit because it does not want to continue with the difficulties I am facing in my life even though they were anticipated in my Life Plan?

The timing of your death is a decision made by your Soul, but your Spirit Guides will do their best to persuade you to continue with your life if you have not yet achieved the goals outlined in your Life Plan. When your Soul goes to the Spirit Side each night, your Spirit Guides will give you warm hugs and a pep talk. They will try to convince you that your Life Plan is still valid, and you will regret missing some important parts of your Life Plan if you take an early exit. Your Spirit Guides will remind you that ending your life in order to avoid an unpleasant situation will not solve the problem since you will likely have to face these difficulties again in a future life, based on what you feel you need to advance your evolution.

In this situation, why would my Spirit Guides allow me to bail out early?

They will not force you to continue with your life because it is the right of your Soul to make its own decisions; however, they will try to persuade your Soul to make decisions that are appropriate for your Life Plan. They know Earth is a very harsh school, and your life can be very difficult at times. They will try to persuade you to persevere and tough it out, knowing that the hardships will eventually pass and your life will become easier to endure.

An analogy here might be helpful. Remember the time your friends sent their daughter to a new boarding school. Part way through the school year, she told them she wanted to leave because her classmates were difficult to live with. Her parents knew that she was going through a rough patch that would not last long. They told their daughter she could leave but only at the end of the school year. Although she was not entirely satisfied with that decision, she decided she could live with it because she could see the light at the end of the tunnel. You know the conclusion to this story: their daughter stayed in the school until the end of the year and managed to work out her problems. With this difficult time behind her, she no longer wanted to leave.

Does this mean that when a girl dies at an early age, her Spirit Guides failed in their persuasion?

Not necessarily. Most times when it appears that a person has died prematurely, it is because that exit point was part of the person's Life Plan, and her Spirit Guides concurred with her decision to exit. On occasion, however, a Soul will ignore the advice of its Spirit Guides and leave a life earlier than originally planned. Each Soul has the final say in this matter, and if a Soul misses something in one life, it can always try again in another life.

How does all this fit in with the tragic events that often happen in our lives? I recall watching a story on a newscast recently about a young boy who died after being run over by a car. His parents could not understand why God would allow such a tragedy to happen. Their little boy had done nothing wrong; he had always been a kind and happy child who had his whole life ahead of him.

Such tragic events are difficult to accept, and the people involved will frequently become angry with God as a result. The reality is that the little boy's Soul decided it was time to leave this incarnation. This could have been part of the Life Plan he created on the Spirit Side, or it may have resulted from a change his Soul made to his Life Plan after he was born. His Soul had good reasons for incarnating as that little boy and then ending his life when he was only four even though these reasons were not apparent to his mom and dad. Perhaps he wanted to experience something that required only four years of life, or maybe he did not

36

need anything for his own evolution and came to Earth to help others (like his parents) with their lives.

A big part of his parents' grief and anguish was the thought that their little boy did not get a chance to live a full life before he died. This seemed very unfair, even cruel, to his parents.

If his parents had understood the truths we have been discussing, they would not have been so upset. If they knew their son was not gone forever and was waiting for them on the Spirit Side, this tragic accident would have been easier to accept. If you send your child off to summer camp, it is natural to be sad to see him leave, and you will miss him while he is gone. You will be comforted, however, by the knowledge that the separation is temporary, and he will be home in a few weeks. Likewise, if you understand that your dead child has crossed over to the Spirit Side and you will be together again when you cross over yourself, you will feel some sadness because of the temporary separation but not the deep grief you would feel if you believed that you would never see him again.

As a follow-up to the first tragedy, a subsequent newscast featured a story about the trial of the drunk driver who had run over this young boy. The driver was convicted and sentenced to three years in jail. The boy's parents were angry at the light sentence this man had received as they felt that justice had not been done. I thought about what had happened, and I wondered why the parents were so upset at this sentence. It was understandable that they were still grieving for their son; however, he was dead and nothing could change that.

It was no doubt coming from a need for retribution. They felt that the drunk driver was wrong and should have to pay for his crime. Such emotions are not necessary, and they do not serve any useful purpose. Their reaction demonstrated a lack of understanding about what had really happened; their son's Soul left this life willingly, and he is now on the Spirit Side waiting to be reunited with his parents when they cross over themselves.

If this could be understood and accepted by all parents in such situations, it would be so much easier for them to deal with such tragedies. Why have you not given this message to everyone else before now?

It all depends on what Souls have set out in their Life Plans and the development stage of the societies they choose for their lives on your planet. Many societies are not yet ready to accept what I have told you, and my message would fall on deaf ears. When your Life Plan was developed, the Wise Ones believed the time was ripe for your society to hear the truths we have been discussing, and we agreed to give you these messages so you can pass them on to others. Some people will accept these truths while many others will reject them. Nevertheless, no matter what happens on Earth, once everyone has died and crossed over to the Spirit Side, the truth will be known to all.

How am I supposed to communicate your truths to everyone else?

You will write a book about our conversations.

Chapter Three

Overcoming Evil

I was taken aback by Albert's prediction that I would write a book about our conversations to propagate his message to others. I had never written a book, and the thought was somewhat daunting. I wondered why Albert did not choose an accomplished author, such as Stephen King or John Grisham, to write his book. Or better yet, why didn't Albert arrange to go on *Oprah* or *Ellen* to convey his message? I concluded that he must have good reasons for his approach, so I decided to continue my conversations with him, hoping that the book-writing task would sort itself out later.

As my first sessions with Albert seemed to raise more questions than they answered, I was keen to keep the dialogue going.

Albert, you said before there is no evil on the Spirit Side, and it is free of all negative emotions. Since all Souls come from the Spirit Side, why are people here often cruel and hurtful to others? Why is there so much pain and suffering on Earth? Why can't Earth be more like the Spirit Side?

If Earth was the same as the Spirit Side, there would be no point for Souls to incarnate on your planet.

Dancing on a Stamp

Earth is part of the universe that is in the realm of lower vibrations and denser matter. It has a very diverse climate, and some areas are extremely harsh for its inhabitants. Humans need oxygen, food, water, and shelter in order to survive, and the absence of any of these can cause discomfort, pain, or death. Earth does not have enough food or clean drinking water for everyone, and this often leads to strife among humans when those who do not have enough of these essentials try to take what they need from other people.

Earth is a school that provides incarnated Souls the opportunity to experience things that do not exist on the Spirit Side. Souls over here do not have to eat, drink, breathe, find shelter, or accumulate wealth or material goods. Likewise, there is no physical discomfort, sickness, or pain on the Spirit Side. Anything a Soul wants on the Spirit Side can be created instantly through *thought creation*—a special process available on the Spirit Side that allows Souls to create things instantly with the power of thought. As a result, there are no shortages of anything on the Spirit Side and no negative emotions. You cannot find anger, envy, or fear on the Spirit Side—only love and happiness.

Earth is a place where Souls can incarnate to experience the harsh physical conditions that exist on your planet, the difficulties that result from these conditions, as well as the negative emotions of humans in response to these factors. The physical hardships arise from the vulnerability of human bodies to injury and disease and the interaction of humans with their

40

physical environment. The negative emotions that people often generate flow from their reactions to these harsh conditions and their interactions with other humans. People feel discomfort or pain if they are hungry or thirsty, or if they are suffering from a disease or injury to their bodies. Fear and anxiety arise when they worry about having enough food and shelter for their families and avoiding injury and disease. Envy and jealousy result when people notice that others have more material goods than they do, which also leads to anger and hate. These negative emotions frequently result in humans doing harmful things to other humans.

Are you saying Earth was designed to be physically harsh to humans with the expectation that they would often react to these conditions in a negative way?

Exactly. Just as a survival school is designed to plunge its students into difficult conditions in order to teach them how to survive and come out alive, Earth was designed as a place for Souls to feel its harsh physical conditions and the negative emotions that result from both a giving and receiving perspective.

One of the main challenges for Souls on Earth is to learn how to control the negative emotions they feel in response to the events that occur every day, including the actions of other people who are struggling to control their own negative emotions. People often inflict harm on others as a negative reaction to injury or disease to their bodies, to their harsh physical conditions, or in response to the actions or emotions of other people. If you are hungry, you might steal bread from another person and inflict bodily harm in the process. The person you stole the bread from might injure you in retaliation. Members of your family, in turn, might seek revenge against this person. And on and on it goes.

So why is there pain and suffering in your world? Humans feel discomfort and pain from their harsh living conditions and from disease or injury to their bodies; this will often lead to negative emotions and harmful actions against other people. People do not have to react negatively to the events around them, but all too often throughout the history of humankind, this has been the result. Human response to negative events is not uniform; some people have learned to control their emotions and seldom cause any harm while others seem to have very little control over their emotions, and they often inflict physical or emotional pain on other humans.

Why would God create a place with so much potential for negative actions?

Earth was created as a place for Souls to face the varied challenges it has to offer, which are not available on the Spirit Side. These challenges provide Souls the opportunity to learn and increase their wisdom, so they can grow and evolve. Souls are fully aware of the conditions on your world before they decide to incarnate, so there are no surprises for them. God expects that Souls who incarnate on Earth will be able to enjoy the all wonderful things Earth has to offer, but He knows they will also have to endure all the bad things that happen on your world. It is all part of the package.

It is similar to human parents on your planet. They do their best to expose their children to all the joyful activities available to humans, such as stroking a kitten, riding a toboggan down a hill, wading into the ocean waves, or smelling the sweet perfume of a rose in bloom. They take great pleasure in watching their children learn and grow from these happy events, but they know, despite all their efforts, they will not be able to shelter their children from all of the distressful or painful events that humans must endure.

As Souls live through all the facets of life in different incarnations, they continue to learn, gain wisdom, and evolve. Most Souls require many lives before they reach a stage where they no longer need to incarnate on your planet in order to evolve to the next level.

It is difficult for people to understand that all Souls are making progress, albeit at different rates. The state of human affairs has changed greatly since they first arrived on Earth. In the early years, primitive men reacted in a very base way to the events around them. They lived in a savage society that was, to quote Thomas Hobbes, "...nasty, brutish, and short." It was typical then for people to become angry with those who stole their food. This often ended in physical altercations. Currently, there are people who have sympathy for this situation, and they will let this crime go without retribution. Today those who control their reactions to such events may have lashed out at the thief in a prior incarnation during the Stone Age. This difference in reactions to that negative event is regarded as progress for those Souls.

Can Souls on the Spirit Side deliberately plan to do harmful acts in their Life Plans?

In most cases, Souls do not plan to do evil deeds in their Life Plans; however, they know this may happen when they respond to the physical and emotional events they will face in their lives. Souls will often include challenging situations or temptations in their Life Plans as a test. They hope they will be able to control their emotions and resist harmful acts, but they know they may fail. A Soul will include challenges in its Life Plan that are appropriate for it, taking into account its level of confidence and its stage of advancement. If a Soul has failed these tests in past lives, it will likely include the temptations in subsequent Life Plans so it can get it right and move on to other things.

Sometimes a Soul will include harmful actions in its Life Plan at the request of another Soul in order to help that other Soul encounter the things it needs in its next life. For example, if a Soul wants to know what it will be like to be abandoned by a parent during childhood, that Soul might ask another Soul in its spirit group to incarnate as a parent in order to fulfill this desire. In this case, the Soul who agreed to be the parent will deliberately include this act of abandonment in its Life Plan.

Most of the time, Souls do not plan to do evil things. Often these result from people veering off course when they make free-will choices in reaction to the events in their lives. This clash of free-will actions often causes turmoil in the lives of those affected, as well as physical or emotional pain in many cases. At times individuals' actions can cause significant deviations in the paths their Souls had hoped to take or in the path that another Soul had planned to follow. Souls know, however, that if they get pushed too far off course, they can come back to Earth another time to try again.

Where does Satan figure into this picture? A number of religions believe the devil is the prime instigator of evil.

Satan does not exist. He was created by religious leaders to be the focal point of all evil, an entity to be feared and vilified. It helped them explain why some very horrible events happened to their followers—they could blame it on the devil. Religions often use the devil as a way to control their members. Their holy men preach that a person must be good and follow the rules of the religion, or the devil will take him away to hell for all eternity. It is to their advantage to keep their congregations fearful of the devil since this will foster frequent attendance at church for protection and salvation.

There is no doubt that evil things happen on Earth, but they are not caused by the devil. Humans can suffer discomfort and pain from disease or injury to their bodies and from interacting with the physical conditions on your planet (such as volcanoes, hurricanes, earthquakes, and fires), which often leads to negative emotions and harmful actions. These factors are the natural consequences of humans living on the planet Earth. The frailty of the human body and the physical conditions of your world are not inherently evil; they are what they are because of the natural evolution of humans and the physical attributes of Earth.

The reactions of humans to the events in their lives do not have to be negative or harmful. Everyone can choose to react in a positive fashion to all the events they encounter.

I am relieved to hear that the devil does not exist. It has occurred to me that Christian holy men have been logically inconsistent with their beliefs about Satan. They have always preached that God is all-powerful, and there is nothing He cannot do. If this is true, how is it that God cannot defeat His archrival, the devil?

Logical consistency has never been a long suit for most Christian holy men. Satan has served a useful purpose in their belief system, and they have been skillful at avoiding questions that have no logical answers. They fervently hope that no one will be brave enough to shout out that the emperor is buck-naked.

Since most of the evil things that happen on this planet are caused by human actions that are often not in accordance with the desires of their Souls, I have a fundamental question for you. Why can't Souls control their human bodies? When a Soul

46

incarnates into a human, why does it seem to be only an observer with the human as the one in charge? Why don't humans follow instructions from their Souls to live according to their Life Plans?

Humans consist of three components: body, mind, and spirit. The body and mind are the physical part of a human, and the Soul is the spirit. As a human, you are fully aware of your body and your mind. Your mind is the thinking and feeling part of you; it controls your body movements and organizes and analyzes all sensory information received by your body. It also originates all emotions and is the storage place for your memories.

Your mind is not consciously aware of your Soul. Your mind receives messages from your Soul in the form of intuitive thoughts and feelings, but it does not always hear or understand these messages. Often when your mind hears a message from your Soul, it does not follow the guidance because it does not understand where the message is coming from, or it concludes that the advice is wrong.

Your Soul is like an observer that occupies your human form (body and mind) during its incarnation. It is able to feel everything your body feels through its physical senses, as well as experience all of the thoughts and emotions that churn through your mind every day. These are all things your Soul came to Earth to experience. When you die and return to the Spirit Side, your mind will merge with your Soul, and your Soul will remember everything that happened during your life. Once back on the Spirit Side, your Soul will again have full access to all the knowledge it had before its incarnation, and it will remember all of its prior lives on Earth. Your Soul will retain your unique personality that has evolved over the course of all your incarnations.

This seems similar to what happened in the movie Avatar, where the Earthling could insert his consciousness into the body of a blue alien and actually become such an alien while in that state. When the alien fell asleep, his consciousness would return to his human body until he once again re-entered the alien body.

Your analogy is close although not entirely accurate. In *Avatar,* the human consciousness fully occupied and controlled the alien body without the presence of an alien mind in the body at the same time. As well, when the human's mind was in the alien body, he retained all the memories of his life as a human, and he knew what he was supposed to accomplish. In real life, your Soul does not have full control of your body—your mind does. Your Soul must try to influence your mind as best it can, which is even more difficult because your mind does not have direct access to all of your Soul's memories of the Spirit Side or of your previous lives

Why can't my Soul exert direct control over my body? Why do I have a mind that seems to operate on its own?

This is all by deliberate design. There would be little point for your Soul to incarnate into a human if it could totally control your body and mind because it would miss most of the challenges it wants to face in this life. For example, if Souls could easily control their human emotions, they would not be able to experience the negative emotions that most humans generate in a typical life.

To make this easier to understand, consider the example of a bullfighter in Spain. When he steps into the ring, he tries to avoid being gored or trampled by the bull through a series of maneuvers with his cape designed to influence the bull's movements. The matador knows the bull might not react in the manner he intends, and he could be gored. But it would make no sense for the matador to enter the ring if he could totally control the bull's movements since there would be no challenge or danger in doing so.

Similarly, Souls, knowing they will not have total control of the human form, incarnate into humans, and that is a significant challenge for them. Souls will try to influence human decisions and actions, but they are not always successful. (The one exception to this mind/Soul relationship is a Soul always makes the final decision regarding the time to end its incarnation and does not need the co-operation of the mind to complete its exit.). Souls that are new to Earth have more difficulty exerting such influence while "old" Souls (i.e., Souls with many previous lives) can do this with greater ease. A woman who lives her life with great love and compassion is likely the incarnation of an old Soul who has learned to be more effective at influencing the actions of her human mind.

If I understand what you are saying, Souls who are incarnate on Earth are at various stages of development on the Earth plane. Some Souls are new to Earth, other Souls have incarnated here numerous times, and, I assume, most Souls are somewhere in between.

Your understanding is correct. It is similar to a school on Earth where some students will be in the first grade, and others will be in eighth grade. The older students will soon graduate to another school while the students in the first grade will continue to progress through the grades until they, too, will graduate. Not all Souls advance through the Earth plane at the same rate. Some Souls can graduate after fewer lifetimes than other Souls. It depends on what a Soul has included in its Life Plans and how quickly the Soul learns to influence and control the humans it occupies.

So a Soul can choose the pace of its learning, like a college student can choose to take less than a full load of classes in any year and graduate later than other students. Why would a Soul choose a longer path to graduation?

Unlike life on Earth, Souls on the Spirit Side are not concerned with a ticking time clock. People on your world are often in a rush, overly concerned about time passing. Most people believe they do not have the luxury of taking seven years to earn a college degree that can be obtained in four years. Humans know their biological clocks are always ticking, and they feel compelled to move through the various stages of their lives quickly, so they will be able to enjoy their lives to the fullest. If students dally too long in college, this will

50

delay the start of their working careers and ability to earn money, buy a house, and have children. If a woman waits too long to have children, her biological clock may make it difficult or even dangerous for her to give birth later in life.

The Spirit Side does not have linear time as it exists on Earth. It makes no difference if a Soul graduates from Earth after fifty-one lives or 234 lives. Souls have "all the time in the world" to live their lives and complete their challenges. As a result, a Soul might choose a slower pace for its evolution, and it will need more incarnations before it graduates.

Personally, the thought that I may have to come back to Earth for more incarnations is somewhat daunting. I find life to be very difficult at times, and such occasions seem to outnumber the good times. When I look back on my life, I am grateful to be where I am right now, and I would not want to go back and live through any of the earlier parts of my life again. So the thought of coming back to Earth after this life to endure yet another life is not very appealing. Who determines when a Soul can graduate from Earth? Is it necessary that all Souls graduate, or can they choose to drop out before they are finished?

Each Soul determines for itself when it has graduated and is ready to move on to adventures elsewhere. The achievements required for graduation are not uniform, and they are not established by God or anyone else on the Spirit Side. Souls can decide to end their Earthly incarnations at any time, even if they have not graduated.

Are there Souls who never leave the Spirit Side to incarnate on Earth?

Yes, there are since each Soul makes its own decision to incarnate after consulting with the Wise Ones and other Souls in its spirit group. Some Souls have already incarnated many times on Earth and have no need to return. Others have found life on your planet so difficult that they choose not to do so again. Still others have never incarnated on Earth and have chosen to remain on the Spirit Side or to incarnate on a different planet.

Is there any way I can convince my Soul to stop coming back here?

Most humans have similar feelings. Once again, you must remember you are viewing things from a human perspective. When you die and cross over to the Spirit Side, you will see things much differently. When viewed from the Spirit Side, the prospect of having more incarnations on Earth is not daunting at all. On the Spirit Side, the typical human life span seems like the blink of an eye. When you leave to incarnate, you know that you will be back on the Spirit Side in no time, and the difficulties you will face will only be a memory. Souls plan their incarnations with a sense of adventure, like people who decide to climb a mountain or run a marathon. They understand that they will endure physical hardships during the course of this activity; however, they are willing to put up with the discomforts in order to reach their goal/s and learn from their journey.

If you really want to avoid coming back to Earth for more lives, you can help yourself through your actions in this life. Although you do not know what your Soul has put into your Life Plan, you can resolve now to respond in a positive manner to all the events in your life, whatever they may be. If you can live your life with lots of love and compassion and learn to control your negative emotions so that you do not inflict physical or emotional harm on others, you will help your Soul progress towards graduation. In other words, if you live your life like a saint, you will help your Soul achieve its goals so it can graduate from the Earth plane.

You make it all sound so easy, but the journey here is no walk in the park. I often wonder what the heck my Soul was thinking when it decided to incarnate once again.

Your Soul knows exactly what it is doing even if your mind does not understand. Earth is a very difficult school and usually only Souls with much experience on the denser planes will dare to take it on. The fact that you are living on Earth now should give you comfort that you are not new to the incarnation cycle. When you finish this life, you can choose not to return to Earth although you will not make that decision until you get back to the Spirit Side when your perspective on things will be very different.

Chapter Four

Crossing Over to the Spirit Side

As I reflected on everything Albert had told me so far, I felt comforted by the knowledge that I would return to the Spirit Side when I died although I still had a lingering concern about the process. Many people die violently in car accidents or other mishaps, some die slowly from terminal cancer, and a few lucky ones die in their sleep. I wondered if the circumstances leading to death made a difference or if it was the same for everyone. For most people, regardless of their beliefs, the prospect of physical death is frightening. I was eager to hear what Albert had to say about death.

I have questions for you, Albert, on the physical death process for humans. One of the concerns I have had since early childhood relates to death and the circumstances that cause death. Will death be painful? Will I be calm and serene or anxious and fearful?

These are questions most people have asked at one time or another. Even those who fervently believe they will go to heaven after they die are often fearful about death.

Let me assure you that physical death and crossing over to the Spirit Side are happy and uplifting experiences for almost everyone, but the transition can vary somewhat from person to person. Most often, Souls will proceed quickly to the Spirit Side once they leave their bodies by passing through a tunnel and heading toward a light. When they emerge from the tunnel, relatives and friends who have already crossed over will greet them warmly. These Souls will appear initially as they did when they were last on Earth so the newly arrived Soul will be able to recognize them immediately. The welcoming party will blanket the Soul with unconditional love to ensure that the transition from Earth to the Spirit Side is joyful and euphoric.

To give you a better idea of what it will be like, imagine you are trudging through a dense forest in the winter, hopelessly lost. It is dark and bitterly cold, and you are walking in knee-deep snow. You are hungry, exhausted, and fearful that you will never find your way out of the forest. Suddenly, you notice a log cabin up ahead with the front door wide open. Standing in the doorway, waving you in, are your parents and grandparents. Behind them in the cabin, you can see a roaring fire in the fireplace, and you can smell the aroma of freshly baked bread and a hearty stew bubbling on the stove. You walk through the door into the warmth of the cabin and the welcoming embrace of your family. You bask in the love that permeates your whole being, and you are very grateful that you are now safely inside the cabin and out of danger. This is similar to the feeling you will enjoy when you die and cross over to the Spirit Side, except your return to the Spirit Side will be much more exhilarating.

Your description of the crossing-over process is reassuring, but I still have a few nagging concerns about my physical death. Will it be painful or distressing?

Regardless of the circumstances of your death, your passing will be peaceful and painless. You may endure pain in your life before you begin your passage; however, once your Soul determines it is time to cross over, you will leave your body before your actual physical death and will not feel any pain or discomfort.

What if I die from injuries I receive in a car accident? Would I not suffer a lot of pain before I actually died?

In this situation, your Soul would know your physical death was about to happen, and you would leave your body just before the crash without feeling the impact or any pain from your injuries. You would watch the final moments of your life from outside of your body without feeling any distress or anxiety, as though you were watching yourself in a movie where everything happens in slow motion. Your body might writhe in pain and cry out in anguish, but your Soul would no longer be present—only your human shell would remain—and you would not have to suffer through these final moments as a human. This will be the case

for every circumstance that might cause your death, no matter how traumatic.

I have often thought that drowning would be a horrible way to die. I can imagine the terror that I would feel as I slipped under the waves—gasping for air as my lungs filled with water.

If you died by drowning, you would not experience the terror you now imagine because your Soul would leave your body before it went under. Even though this may be difficult for you to accept, you must understand that the death of your human body is never painful or distressful, regardless of the events that cause your demise.

You mentioned that I could feel pain in my life before I begin my transition to the Spirit Side. Why am I able to feel pain when I am not in the process of dying?

Pain is one of the realities you live with as a human just as hunger and thirst are things you might encounter in your life. All of these physical discomforts, as well as the emotional ones, such as hatred, anger, and fear, are present to some degree in most human lives. Your Soul might need to endure pain to complete its knowledge and advance its evolution. (Recall my analogy of the child in Kenya who had knowledge of extreme cold but needed to go to Alaska in January in order to feel the cold. Since there is no physical or emotional pain on the Spirit Side, the only way for you to understand pain fully is to experience it on Earth). People who are living with

pain do not consciously choose to endure pain, but their Souls have made that choice. The reasons will only become apparent once they have crossed over to the Spirit Side.

You said the transition to the Spirit Side could vary somewhat from person to person. Is it ever unpleasant?

In a few cases the transition can be unpleasant, depending on the person's beliefs prior to death. On the Spirit Side, Souls can create their own environment and change it whenever they want by *thought creation*. There are people who have very strong beliefs about what will happen to them after they die, and this might cause them to create an environment for themselves immediately after death that fulfills these expectations.

For example, those with strong convictions that they will go to hell after they die might create such a place waiting for them after death. This would last for a short time only as their Spirit Guides would be there to persuade them that God did not condemn them to this place, and they can leave at any time. Once they understand this message, they will leave this "hell" and move on to a happier place on the Spirit Side. Very few Souls undergo this temporary unpleasantness—it happens only to those people who stubbornly refuse to accept the realities of the Spirit Side so that they can cling to their Earthly beliefs. These Souls are not left to flounder aimlessly in such

places. Eventually they make the full transition to the love and happiness of the Spirit Side.

I accept what you have said about physical death and the transition to the Spirit Side, but I still am still apprehensive about the process. To me, it is like stepping through a doorway into a deep, dark abyss. I will not know what is on the other side or what will happen next.

A good friend of mine recently went through a very scary period in his life. The lab test results from his annual physical showed anomalies in his blood, which could be associated with myeloma (bone cancer). While he waited for the results of the additional tests his doctor requested (which eventually came back negative), he was very preoccupied with the prospect that he might have myeloma. I tried my best to give him comfort and encouragement and told him not to worry. He listened to me politely and then said, "That's easy for you to say. You're not the one facing terminal cancer."

When I thought about what he had said, I had to acknowledge to myself that he was right. I would have had a different perspective if I were the one who was facing death. This would be still be true, Albert, even in light of what you told me about what happens after death. Why is it so hard for humans to contemplate their own deaths?

A large part of it has to do with the physical form of a human, consisting of a body and a mind. Instinctively, humans, like most animals, have a strong desire to survive. Humans also have the added layer of their thinking and feeling minds, which can contemplate the

future and anticipate events to come. The human mind has trouble comprehending what happens to it when its physical body dies. The mind becomes so attached to its body that it is difficult for it to contemplate leaving its body behind to rot in its grave. This is true even for those people who believe their Souls will leave their bodies on death and go to heaven. No matter what their beliefs, humans will always have a nagging doubt in the back of their minds that maybe they have it all wrong, and they will not survive death.

This is very normal, and it is an important part of human life on your planet. The uncertainty about what happens to you at death and where you go after that often fosters fear and anxiety, which can lead to other negative emotions during your life. Your challenge is to try to stare down your fears by reminding yourself every day that you are an immortal Soul, and your death is actually a doorway leading to the Spirit Side.

What about judgment after death? As you know, most religions believe we must meet our maker after we die, and He will pass judgment on us based on how we lived our lives. If we were bad, we will be banished to hell to suffer in pain forever. If we were good, we will be allowed to enter heaven to enjoy a pleasant and blissful existence.

These religions are wrong because hell does not exist, and no one judges you after you die, except yourself. God does not judge Souls based on what they did in their lives, nor does He banish them to a horrible place if they have been bad. All Souls are all part of God, and it would make no sense for God to exile parts of Himself to an awful place for eternity. Unlike His portrayal by many religions, God is not like an Earthly king who sits on a gold throne dispensing rewards or punishments to people after they die. God is not vain or vengeful, and He does not need or expect people to worship Him in a certain manner, or at all. God does not make rules for people to follow, and He does not punish Souls for their actions, no matter what they have done. Just as parents on your planet would not forever abandon their five-year-old child for misbehaving, God does not banish the Souls who have misbehaved. God gave you free will to make choices in your life, and sometimes you will exercise your free will in a negative and harmful way. This is all part of life as a human, and God knows this will happen often.

If God did not want you to be able to stray off course, He could have taken away your free will or stopped you from incarnating on Earth in the first place. God knows a few Souls will be saints, others might become cruel monsters, and most will be somewhere in between. The variety of circumstances that Souls encounter during their lives provides God the opportunity to experience life on Earth from many different perspectives.

If there is no hell, what happens to all the murderers when they die?

They cross over to the Spirit Side like everyone else.

Most people would consider that result to be a grave injustice. How is it possible these criminals can end up in the same place as Mother Theresa?

Once again, your Earthly perspective taints your view of things. In your secular world, you have laws to maintain the peace for all citizens. These laws help to make societies civilized in contrast to the "law of the jungle" that would otherwise prevail. In order for this system to work, there must be sanctions for those who break the laws, such as fines or prison terms. If murderers were not punished for their crimes, most people would be very upset, concluding that justice had not been done.

As well, most religions have adopted the belief that there will be punishment in the afterlife for those who do not obey God's laws. Like the secular system, this is intended to provide their members with a sense of justice—because all the bad people will be punished in the hereafter—and a strong incentive to be good and follow the rules of the religion.

On the Spirit Side, it is acknowledged that humans will sometimes stray off course when they exercise their free will; however, this does not justify punishment for those persons who do so since it is all part and parcel of a life on Earth. When Souls cross

63

over to the Spirit Side, they are always genuinely sorry for the negative things they did, and they will always strive to understand how they might have avoided such actions.

If no one will be punished after death, why would someone want to live a good life? Misbehaving can be much more fun than staying on the straight and narrow.

There are good reasons that most humans strive to be good. The first is that all people have an inner sense of what is right and wrong, and they feel a moral imperative to do what is right. Most people would not abuse a child or murder another human even if there was no punishment on Earth or after death for doing so. These people prefer to do good deeds because it feels like the right thing to do. This *gut feeling* about what is right and wrong does vary somewhat from person to person and from culture to culture although most of the main principles are consistent. These moral guidelines arise from unconscious residual memories of the Spirit Side and from messages sent to them from their Souls and Spirit Guides.

The second reason is that most people believe they will have to account for their actions after they die. Almost all humans believe that God will judge them for their actions, and He will reward or punish them accordingly while others believe that karma will make them pay for their misdeeds in a future life. The people who accept my truths will know that both of these beliefs are wrong, but they will still strive to be good in order to fulfill the aspirations of their Souls.

I still have trouble accepting that murderers end up in the same place as the good people. Surely they must pay for their sins.

Life on your planet is a way for Souls to learn and evolve without any concern about retribution or punishment. Murderers do not go to the Spirit Side as a reward for their crimes; they go to the Spirit Side because there is no other place to go. All Souls start out from the Spirit Side and return there when they die, regardless of what kind of life they lived on your planet. Murderers will have a difficult time conducting their life reviews as they will then fully understand the pain and suffering they inflicted on others, for which they will be very remorseful. Other Souls will not criticize or shun murderers, and no one will punish them for their actions. In fact, the victims will embrace them with love and compassion and forgive them unconditionally for what they did. After this, murderers will be eager to return to Earth in another life so they can make amends and live a better life the next time around.

What happens in a life review?

After you have crossed over to the Spirit Side and have completed your transition, you will begin your life review with the help of your Spirit Guides. Your life review will allow you to view all aspects of your

65

life in whatever order you prefer—with plenty of pauses to allow you to reflect on your actions and discuss their implications with your Spirit Guides and the Wise Ones. You can choose to see your life as though you were back in your Earthly body and re-living the events, or you can view the events in your life as though you were watching yourself in a 3-D movie. You will be able to feel other peoples' emotions in response to your words and actions.

For example, if you said mean and cruel things to someone, you will be able to feel the pain this person felt in response to your words. On the other hand, if you shoveled your elderly neighbors' driveway after a snowstorm, you would feel their deep gratitude for your kind deed as they watched you through their front window. Your life review will give you a better understanding of how your words and actions affected others, and this will help you prepare for your next incarnation. You will also have full recall of the Life Plan you devised before your incarnation, and you will be able to see how closely you followed your intended path.

I can see how a life review could become uncomfortable in places. I think most of us do not really understand how our actions affect others or the full extent of the pain we have caused other people. How do we move forward after our life review?

The purpose of your life review is not to make you feel guilty but to help you understand how your actions affected others. **Your life review will demonstrate the pain and suffering you inflicted on others, and it will give you an opportunity to understand how you could have avoided these acts. This will help you to grow as a Soul and prepare you for your next life.**

Will anyone give me a grade or score on the life I have completed?

You are the only one who will judge your performance in this life. You will explore all aspects of your life with your Spirit Guides and with the other Souls who had significant roles in your life, like your parents, siblings, spouse, and children. They will be present during your life review, and you will be with them during their life reviews; however, they will not judge you, and you will not judge them. Instead, everyone will strive to offer advice and guidance to everyone else in a spirit of mutual co-operation.

Thank God I will not have to meet St. Peter at the pearly gates after I pass on. (Maybe now I can get rid of the fireproof body suit I keep in my closet!) Personally, I think it is a good idea to follow the wisdom spelled out in a piece of graffiti I saw during my college days: "Don't judge another man until you have walked a mile in his shoes (because, by then, you are a mile away and you've got his shoes)."

Very funny. Although I am not allowed to discuss the details of your Life Plan, I can tell you it is not in the cards for you to become a comedian—for obvious reasons.

Chapter Five

Flying in the Face of the Church

After my first sessions with Albert, my head was spinning. The things he told me about why I was here and what would happen to me when I died flew in the face of almost everything I had been taught as a child, growing up in a very religious Roman Catholic family. The Catholic Church told us that God was the Supreme Being who put all of us on Earth—for some purpose known only to Him—to live in accordance with His rules, which were conveyed to us by the leaders of the Catholic Church. After we died, we would appear before God to receive His judgment. If we had been good and had followed all of His rules, God would let us enter heaven, where we would enjoy a blissful existence forever. If we had been bad and had breached His rules, He would send us to an awful place called hell, where we would suffer in excruciating pain for all eternity.

As I reflected on my Catholic upbringing, I recalled that many of the Church's rules dictated the requirements for the proper worship of God, such as attending holy Mass every Sunday, partaking of the holy sacraments, like Communion and Confession, on a regular basis, and fasting on Good Friday. These rules did little to encourage a people to live a better life in society, but if you broke the rules, you could end up in hell, even if you were good in every other respect. As a teenager, I

69

struggled with the Catholic Church's position that people could live good lives, full of love, kindness, and compassion for others, and yet if they did not belong to the Catholic Church and follow its rules, they would go to hell when they died. On the other hand, those who was cruel and hurtful to others for most of their lives could end up in heaven as long as they followed the rules of the Catholic Church and confessed their sins before they died. This outcome made no sense to me.

The Catholic Church's rules relating to worship were often arbitrary and illogical. Members were obligated to attend Mass every Sunday, and the failure to do so was a mortal sin, punishable by an eternity in hell—unless this sin was forgiven in Confession. If a person went to Mass every day from Monday to Saturday but missed going on Sunday, the result was the same. With this rule, the Church seemed to be telling us that form was more important than substance, and God preferred people who attended church service only once a week, provided it was on Sunday, over those who went to Mass every day of the week but missed Sunday. I will never understand this rule.

I received my initial indoctrination to the beliefs of the Catholic Church in a two-week catechism course designed to prepare its students for their First Communion. This class, which was mandatory for all children in the parish who had just completed the first grade, was a very unwelcome intrusion into our first summer break from school. The teachers followed Catholic tradition and did their best to drum into our heads as much Catholic dogma as time permitted. In the process, they managed to destroy the innocence of our youth by telling us that we were all sinners, and we had to confess our sins to the priest before receiving Holy Communion for the first time.

Like the other kids in the class, I hadn't thought of myself as a sinner until that summer—likely because I didn't really know much about the Church's concept of sin. I soon found out the Church had a very long list of things that were sins, slotted into two categories: mortal sins (for the serious offenses) and venial sins (for the minor infractions).

The most troubling part of the class dealt with the punishment that God would hand out after we died if we had sins on our Souls. For mortal sins, we would be sent to hell, where we would suffer in its raging fires for eternity. If we had only venial sins on our Souls, God would make us serve time in purgatory (which was a place similar to hell) until our Souls had been cleansed of our sins, and we were allowed to enter heaven. To a seven-year-old child, the thought of punishment in one of these places was terrifying as I remembered the pain I felt the previous Christmas when I had passed my hand too close to a burning candle.

After scaring the heck out of us with the prospect of purgatory and hell, they tried to provide a little solace by encouraging us to say a short prayer, a plea for God's mercy, every night before we went to sleep:

> *Now I lay me down to sleep,*
> *I pray the Lord my Soul to keep.*
> *If I should die before I wake,*
> *I pray the Lord my Soul to take.*

The third line really got my attention; I realized then that I could die in my sleep one night and never again see my mom and dad or my brother and sisters. And if I happened to have

71

sins on my Soul when I died, I would be sent to purgatory or hell. Until they taught me to recite that little prayer, it had never occurred to me that I could die at any time; I had always believed death was something that happened only to old people. There were many nights after that when I was terrified to fall asleep, fearful I might never wake up again. In the years that followed, the fear I learned that summer hung over me like a dark cloud, and I can remember many mornings on my way to school when I would silently recite the Hail Mary over and over again with the hope that my prayers would be answered, and I would be allowed to live a little longer.

As I recalled these events as an adult, I had difficulty understanding what was the Church trying to accomplish by instilling so much fear into a group of young children. Sadly, I concluded that the Church had always used guilt and fear to control its members, and they likely believed that this worked best if they started the process at an early age.

Shortly after my First Communion, my parents enrolled me as an altar boy, which they thought was quite an honor. In those days, the Catholic Mass was conducted in Latin, and altar boys "served Mass" by assisting the priest during the service, including responding to the Latin prayers recited by the priest. As part of my preparation for this role, I was given a booklet containing the phonetic pronunciation of these Latin prayers, which I had to memorize so I could respond properly to the priest.

When I think about this, it seems odd this booklet did not provide the English translations of these prayers, only the phonetic guides on pronunciation. As I recited these prayers in Latin each Sunday at Mass, I had no idea what the words meant. But this did not seem to concern the priest or the congregation; everyone was content that I was following the age-old traditions of the Catholic Church even if no one except the priest understood the prayers. So much for the idea that prayer was supposed to be a thoughtful communication with God.

Serving as an altar boy at Mass each Sunday did not make me feel any holier or closer to God. It was mostly a matter of dressing up in red and white vestments, mumbling Latin prayers at the appropriate time, and assisting the priest with all the pomp and ceremony that formed the basis of every Mass. Several parts of the Mass did have obvious connections with historic symbolism although most of it seemed to be a meaningless series of prayers, gestures, and pageantry. I often wondered if there was something wrong with me since I did not feel any noticeable uplifting of my spirits while I was serving Mass.

One of the few interesting parts of serving Mass occurred during Holy Communion when the priest dispensed a host, which represented the body and blood of Jesus Christ, to those parishioners who chose to partake of this sacrament. The host was a thin, round wafer of unleavened bread that only the priest could touch after it was consecrated. In order to receive the host, individuals knelt at the Communion railing at the front of the church and stuck out their tongues when the priest approached. After the priest had placed a host on their outstretched tongues, the individuals would retract the hosts back into their mouths and then carefully stick the host on the roof of the mouth until it dissolved. At that time, it was a sin to chew the host or even touch it with your teeth.

One of my duties as an altar boy was to follow the priest as he dispensed the hosts. I held a small brass plate under each person's chin to catch the host in case it slipped off a person's tongue. From this vantage point, I was able to see a great variety of human tongues of all sizes, shapes, and colors— things most people never get to see. Many tongues were long and narrow while others were broad and flat. Some were pink, a few had a purplish tinge, and the odd one had a sickly white coating, which made me think they had not been anywhere near toothpaste or mouthwash in a long time. The funniest ones had purple veins protruding from underneath. Most times I had to bite my lip to keep from smiling. If those people only knew what their tongues looked like, they would have left the Church to join another religion. Since those days, the Catholic Church has changed its policies; it now allows people to receive the host in the palm of one hand and use the other hand to insert it into their mouth.

My focus on tongues during Communion proved to be costly one Sunday. I was following the priest back and forth along the Communion railing with my little brass plate when the unthinkable happened: a host slipped off someone's tongue, hit the edge of my plate, and fell to the floor. The priest stopped abruptly and waved his arms to silence the choir while everyone else in the congregation froze in their tracks. It was almost as if I had spilled a radioactive isotope from its lead container. The priest sent me to the sacristy to fetch a little black valise he kept on the shelf. He pulled out a little brass shovel and a small black brush and very carefully whisked the host onto his little shovel. He then used the brush and shovel to scoop up everything on the floor within a six-inch radius of where the host had landed. I assumed his goal was to ensure that no little pieces of Christ were left behind because who knows what God would have done if someone had later stepped on His son. Thankfully, the priest was able to retrieve every last molecule that may have fragmented from the host when it hit the floor, thereby sparing us all from the wrath of God.

When I reached my teens, I stopped serving Mass and got to sit in the pews with my family every Sunday. At that point, Mass was conducted in the vernacular, and the parishioners could respond to all the prayers in English. Despite this change, all the same pomp and pageantry remained, and Mass was no more meaningful to me than before. One of the worst parts was the homily when the priest would preach to the congregation. Most of the time these sermons were boring, and it was difficult to stay focused without zoning out. I do remember one occasion, however, when the sermon had a bit of spice to it, especially for a teenager.

On this particular Sunday, the priest startled everyone with a revelation about what had transpired recently during someone's confession. (Confession in the Catholic Church was the procedure that gave its members an opportunity to confess their sins to the priest in strict confidence and receive forgiveness for all their transgressions). Without naming the person, the priest told the congregation that a man had confessed the sin of being impure with his wife. Even though the priest did not spell it out, everyone knew the man was talking about sexual activities. Much to my disappointment, the priest did not provide any details on what this man had done, but he did go on to reassure everyone that there was nothing a husband and wife could do to each other that was impure, and there was no need to confess these activities.

My imagination immediately kicked into high gear. *What exactly had this man and his wife done*, I wondered. I discretely scanned the congregation, hoping to find someone squirming a little, but it seemed like almost everyone was slightly uncomfortable. My eyes settled on a very attractive young woman sitting in the pew in front of me as I wondered wistfully if she might be game to try out a few of these impure activities one night in the back seat of my car.

As the congregation filed out of the church at the end of the Mass, I detected a few sly smiles on some of the men. No doubt they were anticipating going to bed that night, armed with this new assurance from the priest that they were free to engage in all sorts of sexual activities with their wives without any concern that such acts would be impure or sinful.

In those days the Church had a multitude of rules prohibiting or restricting sexual activity. When I was a young teenager, barely past puberty, the priest advised the congregation one Sunday that he was holding a "character building" session for the teenage boys of the parish. My parents insisted that I attend this class, and they dropped me off at the priest's rectory at the appointed time where I joined a small group of my classmates whose parents were of like mind. None of us knew what "character building" meant until the priest began his lecture. The purpose of the meeting was to warn us that "self-pleasuring" activities were sinful and offensive to God. Although he did not use the word "masturbation," we all knew what he meant. In the event we succumbed to this temptation, the priest told us we had to confess this sin as soon as possible. As an aside, he told us that sometimes we might have a "wet dream" during our sleep, but this was not a sin as long as we did not continue to enjoy the sexual fantasy from this dream after we woke up. To make it easier for us to confess this sin, the priest gave us a code phrase to use; we could tell him we had "spilled the seeds," and he would know what we meant. As I thought about what the priest had said, I remembered what my good friend Mark had recently confided to me. Since people going to Confession were expected to tell the priest how long it had been since their last Confession and how many times they had sinned, I shuddered to think of how embarrassing it would be for Mark to confess that he had "spilled the seeds" eleven times in the past week.

The Catholic Church not only tried to control one's actions, but one's thoughts as well. The Church regarded impure thoughts (i.e., thoughts about sex) as a grave sin against God that would blacken our Souls. Since most of us found it difficult to block out all the different thoughts that popped into our heads every day, this sin was very hard to avoid.

This brings to mind an amusing story from my college days. My good friend John had fallen in love with a very attractive young woman who happened to be a devout Catholic. Needless to say, she faithfully followed the Church's laws against sexual intercourse before marriage, so it was a platonic relationship to that point, much to John's dismay. As a pre-condition to their expected marriage, John had to "turn Catholic," which required him to take instructions from a priest about the Church and its beliefs and then be baptized as a Catholic. During the course of these instructions, the priest told him that having impure thoughts was a serious sin that had to be confessed without delay. The first time John went to Confession, his girlfriend went with him to the church for moral support. John entered the confessional and recited his sins to the priest, including several episodes of having impure thoughts about his sweetheart. After leaving the confessional, and feeling good that he had wiped his slate clean, he sat down in the pew next to his companion. Before he could stop himself, he noticed how enticing she looked in her short skirt and tight-fitting sweater. In the blink of an eye, he was back on the slippery slope to hell. *Now what?* he wondered. He could go back into the confessional and confess this new impure thought, but he would have to explain to his girlfriend why he needed another turn. Besides, as long as she was in the church, the cycle would likely repeat when he got out. John sadly concluded that being a good Catholic was not going to be easy.

Even though a few of these memories brought a smile to my face, most were still very troubling. And I found out recently one day at the gym that I was not the only one who had issues with his Catholic upbringing. I was walking briskly on a treadmill that morning when a tall, slim man got on the machine next to me. He introduced himself as David, and we exchanged a few comments about the weather. I noticed he was reading an article with an unusual headline: "Avoid 'misuse of sex' in marriage, Canadian bishops warn."

"My God," David suddenly exclaimed, "Will you listen to those old fools. They have never had sex themselves, but they are trying to tell married couples what they should not do in their own bedrooms."

As I turned to look at David, with my eyebrows raised, he told me the article he was reading was a story about the Canadian Conference of Catholic Bishops releasing a pastoral letter warning married couples to avoid sexual acts that were not chaste, since such activities were contrary to God's intentions.

"Sorry about my knee-jerk reaction," he explained as he handed me the article, "but I am a recovering Catholic." He said it the same way someone would admit he was a recovering drug addict. I had no immediate response, but after reading the news story, I invited David for a coffee after the workout so I could ask him about his outburst.

I learned that David, who was in his late fifties, had a childhood similar to mine. He also grew up in a religious Roman Catholic family and had served Mass in his parish church for several years. He told me the Church taught him all the same rules and beliefs I had learned, and he had swallowed all of them "hook, line, and sinker." By the time he was in college, however, he began to question these beliefs, which he found to be lacking in many respects.

"The final tipping point came when I read the *Conversations with God* books," he recalled, "especially the chapter in Book 2 where Neale Walsch cleverly mocks some of the key elements of the Church's dogma. When I finished reading this chapter, everything suddenly became very clear—as though I had been sitting in the dark for years, and then somebody flicked on the light. I was finally able to recognize all the rules and beliefs of the Church that were arbitrary, illogical, or even silly, with most of them doing nothing to encourage their members to be better citizens in society. For the most part, these rules were just tools for the Church to control its members with guilt and fear. I call myself a recovering Catholic because I am still struggling to undo the effects of all the guilt and fear I accumulated over the years as a result of believing the nonsense the Church taught me when I was young."

"A good example of a belief that seemed to defy all logic was the Church's doctrine on Original Sin," he continued. "In catechism we were taught that all humans were born with Original Sin on their Souls, which arose from the transgressions committed by Adam and Eve. Even though infants were incapable of doing anything wrong, they came into this world with their Souls blackened by this sin. The Church preached that no one with Original Sin on his Soul could enter heaven, and a person had to be baptized as a Catholic to get rid of this sin."

"I recall the same teachings from my catechism class," I responded, " and I have always thought that this belief had a fundamental flaw—it was the same as punishing children for crimes committed by their father, a concept that has no validity whatsoever."

"There is no doubt in my mind that this belief was flawed. It was contrary to natural justice, and it offended our inherent sense of fairness," David agreed. "It meant that an un-baptized baby who died suddenly would be shut out of heaven because of a sin he did not commit. After reflecting on this doctrine in recent years, however, I have discerned the real purpose for this rule—it provided a compelling reason for Catholic parents to have their babies baptized as soon as possible after birth. Once enrolled in the Church, it was expected that they would continue as faithful members, marry other good Catholics, and produce many babies who would all become practicing Catholics. It was a great way for the Church to ensure a steady flow of new members."

"I know where you are coming from, but things have changed since we were children. The Church has made progress," I countered.

"This is true," he conceded, "but they still have a long way to go. The news story about the letter from the Bishops is a good example of how the Church still tries to exert control over its members over things that should not concern them. Do these guys really think anyone out there—other than a small minority of sycophantic Catholics—will pay any attention to what they say about the sexual practices of married couples? Are they doing themselves more harm than good by preaching that God wants husbands and wives to be 'chaste' in their bedrooms? (And does anyone really know what 'chaste' actually means?) In any event, my sympathy goes out to those people who might take this letter to heart. Think of how much unnecessary guilt these bishops have created for those couples who will now reflect on the sex they have come to enjoy and wonder if they have offended God. And all this pontificating is coming from the same group who haven't been able to prevent their own priests from sexually abusing children."

"I would guess that the vast majority of young adults in our society, as well as most of the older ones, will ignore this pastoral letter without giving it a second thought," I responded. "But your point about sexually abusive priests really hits close to home. Several years ago I was dismayed to hear that the priest who had served as the pastor of my home parish when I was in high school had been convicted of five counts of gross indecency relating to the sexual abuse of five teenage boys. I was even more upset when I realized these incidents had occurred during his tenure at our parish and that I had served Mass with two of the victims. I thought it was ironic that this priest, who had often lectured the teenagers in the parish against pre-marital sex, had been at the same time sexually abusing young boys in his rectory."

"I am sorry to hear that," David said.

"So was I since two of those guys were my friends," I lamented. "I have often wondered since then why it took so long for the victims to come forward."

"It is not a surprise to me," David countered. "In those days most adults of my parents' generation thought priests could do no wrong, so it is unlikely anyone would have believed the victims even if they had found the courage to report the abuse when it happened."

"I know what you mean," I agreed. "The Catholic clergy in those days were all held in very high esteem. I can still recall the occasions when the bishop came to our parish for Confirmation. He was treated like royalty; after the Mass, there was always a small group of people milling around him, waiting for an opportunity to genuflect and kiss his ring."

"Sometimes, even today, you will find bishops who long for the old days when everyone listened to them without question," David continued. "I remember an incident that happened a few years ago in my home city. Many of the Catholic schools had been raising money by sponsoring bingos and casinos (which were licensed by the government) to help fund school programs and field trips. Then one day the local bishop decided that such fund-raising activities were immoral and contrary to Catholic principles. Despite the fact that the Catholic School Trustees, who had all been elected by the taxpayers, voted in favor of allowing the schools to continue raising funds this way since they knew it would not be easy to find other sources to replace this money, this bishop, who had not been elected by anyone, would not relent; he threatened to boycott the Board's annual opening meeting and blacklist any school that continued this practice. The worst part of this whole episode is that the Trustees caved in and followed the bishop's orders. Now I can understand why some Americans were concerned during the 1960 presidential election that John F. Kennedy might have to follow orders from the Pope."

I did not know how to respond to David's tirade since I found it hard to disagree with most of what he said, so I decided to revisit his earlier points about the rules of the Church. "I understand where you are coming from regarding the arbitrary and illogical rules of the Church, but other religions also have rules that do not make any sense—like the ones that prohibit dancing, drinking caffeine, eating pork, or require men to wear a turban or women to cover their faces when they are out in public. I could go on and on, but I think you get my point."

"I know the Catholic Church isn't the only religion with these kinds of rules," he conceded, "but it is the religion I am most familiar with. I still don't understand why more people don't realize that most of these rules were established as a way for these religions to control their members and keep them in the fold."

"As several authors have already noted," I replied, "it is easier for people to believe what they have been taught by their parents and religious leaders than to analyze these teachings in light of their own life experiences and establish their own beliefs. Most people are content to follow the easy path and not rock the boat."

"I think you are right, but it is not our problem. I am glad we had this chat. It's comforting to know there are others who share my views," he concluded as he ambled out the door.

As I left the gym to head home, I thought about what David had said and how Albert had blasted big holes in almost everything the Church had taught me when I was young. I knew I had to raise the issue with Albert.

Albert, almost everything you have told me so far contradicts what the Catholic Church taught me when I was young. How is it that Catholic Church, which has been around for centuries with millions of followers, can be so far off course?

To some extent, the Catholic Church developed its beliefs in order to fulfill the needs of its followers over the history of the Church. In earlier times, almost everyone would have rejected the truths I have passed on to you, and any attempt to enlighten the people would have been a wasted effort. The core message I have given you will not be accepted by everyone, but I hope there will be open-minded people today who are searching for truths they cannot find in organized religion, and who will thus embrace what I have said.

The Catholic Church has a long history, and most of its practices and beliefs have been in place since its early days. Many of its rules were developed centuries ago when most citizens followed the laws established by their ruling despot without asking questions. In this

fertile ground, the Church knew it could persuade its members to follow its rules even if they were arbitrary or illogical. In current times many of its members are skeptical about these rules; however, changes are slow to come—mainly because the Church's religious leaders are not inclined to listen to their members or to revisit matters that have been part of its history for so long. The Church does not honor democratic principles; it is governed by the Pope with help from the cardinals and the bishops, who do not want lay members to participate in the election or appointment of Church leaders or have any input on changes to the rules or beliefs of the Church. It is to their distinct advantage to keep all the power to themselves, and this is not likely to change anytime soon.

How does the Church justify this system of governance?

As you know, the Pope is the supreme leader of the Roman Catholic Church. On the death of the Pope, the College of Cardinals meets to choose one of their own to be the new Pope. Cardinals are selected by the Pope from the members of the College of Bishops, who are also appointed by the Pope. The Catholic Church believes that God works through the College of Cardinals to choose the Pope as His spokesman on Earth. They assert that this makes the Pope infallible since whatever he decrees is actually coming from God. Questioning the dictates of the Pope is tantamount to questioning God. Under this system, which has been in place since the early days of the Church, there is no room for democracy. It is not possible for the lay members of the Church to elect the

Pope because God must choose the Pope, and, according to the holy men of the Church, God only works with the cardinals when He chooses a new Pope.

This seems similar to the Divine Right of Kings theory used by some European monarchs centuries ago to justify their claim that their authority should not be challenged because they were chosen by God.

The similarities are certainly there. Historically, one of the best ways for a despot to maintain power was to convince the people he derived his authority from God, and his wishes and commands were sanctioned by God. To the extent this was accepted, the citizens were reluctant to challenge his authority, no matter how illogical, inconsistent, or harmful his dictates might be. After all, how could he be wrong if he was appointed by God?

The religious leaders of the Catholic Church have always taken full advantage of this paradigm. The Pope, the cardinals, and the bishops enjoy their positions of authority in the Church and the power this gives them over all its members. Since they claim their authority is derived directly from God, who communicates His desires through them, they are not inclined to listen to the lay members of the Church— who obviously, at least to them, do not have the same direct pipeline to God.

Is this true? Does God speak to the Pope and the cardinals?

God does speak to the Pope and the cardinals but not exclusively. God speaks to everyone, and no person or group of persons has a monopoly on these messages. God will often speak through your Soul or your Spirit Guides. Often He sends Masters (who are very advanced Souls) to your planet to live amongst humans in order to spread His message. Jesus, Moses, Krishna, Buddha, and Muhammad are a few of the prominent Masters who have walked the Earth to help humans with their journeys. There have been other Masters who deliberately kept low profiles when they lived on your planet, and there are Masters living on Earth right now who have chosen to stay out of the limelight.

If God speaks to everyone, why do humans disagree on so many things? Does God send out conflicting messages?

God's core message to humans is always the same: feel only love for yourself and all other humans and creatures, and know that whatever you do to others, you also do to yourself. Although everyone gets the same message from God, some people do not hear it because they are not listening while others hear the message but choose to ignore it because it conflicts with their earthly desires.

Is it true that all the rules and beliefs of the Catholic Church, decreed by a long line of Popes since the beginning of the Church, actually came directly from God?

God does not dictate rules or beliefs for humans to follow, whether religious or otherwise. God's messages always deal with the highest truths, and He does not try to control the day-to-day actions of humans. He gave mankind the right to exercise free will, and He will not interfere with that right. For this reason, God did not dictate the rules and beliefs of the Catholic Church or any other religion. They all sprang forth from the minds of holy men who were able to convince others that they spoke on behalf of God.

What about Jesus Christ, the founder of the Catholic Church? Did he originate the dogmas of the Church?

Jesus was the foundation for the Catholic Church, which developed after his death, but he did not prescribe all of its rules and beliefs. Jesus was a Master who incarnated as a human in order to spread God's message to humans and lead them to a higher level of consciousness. Jesus was and still is a son of God—just as all Souls are children of God. Jesus was a very advanced Soul who did not need to experience anything himself; he incarnated solely to help others through his teachings. While it is true that Jesus originated the Catholic Church, he did not dictate the myriad of rules and beliefs the Church has developed over the centuries. You will not find anywhere in the scriptures that Christ told his followers they had to attend Mass every Sunday, partake of Holy Communion at least once a year, confess their sins in Confession, or abstain from eating meat on Fridays (a former rule that has been repealed), to mention a few of the rules of the Church, past and present. Nor did he prescribe the procedures for the worship of God or the governing structure of the Church. All of these rules were developed by the holy men who lead the Church after Christ's death.

What about the Bible? Most Christians believe this book represents the word of God.

God did not dictate the Bible; it was written by men who were all following their own agendas, as were the holy men since then who cited passages from the Bible to justify the rules and beliefs that they advocated for their religions. Many of the original texts that comprise the Bible were later altered by religious leaders to suit their own purposes. Numerous scriptures in the New Testament are now very different from the original versions. In the early days of the Church, its religious leaders agreed, after considerable debate, on a set of beliefs for their religion, and they re-wrote and edited parts of the original passages from the New Testament to ensure that the scriptures that survived conformed to their vision of the Church. Often they deliberately concealed or destroyed scriptures that contradicted the beliefs they had established for the Church. As a result, the Bible that you know today was written by many different men (and revised by the holy men who followed them), and it does not represent the "word of God" as various holy men have claimed over the centuries.

Why have you not revealed your truths to the Church leaders?

You can well imagine what would happen to the Church if its leaders and members accepted the truths I have been telling you. The principal beliefs of the Church would no longer have any validity, and it would cease to exist in its current form. Without millions of members to follow their commands and make monetary contributions to the Church coffers, the Pope, the cardinals, and the bishops would lose their power base. This is clearly not in their interests, so they will continue to do whatever they can to maintain their assertion that a person can only enter heaven if she belongs to the Catholic Church and faithfully adheres to its rules and beliefs as decreed by the Pope. The Church's holy men will always try to discredit any theories or beliefs that are contrary to the dogmas of the Church, so the truths I have been passing on to you will be vehemently rejected by them as heresy.

This is not to say the Catholic Church does not have its good points. For the most part, its leaders are well-intentioned, and they do encourage their members to obey the Ten Commandments and honor the Golden Rule. The Church also does good deeds in the world through its charitable activities. Sometimes, however, its rules cause unnecessary hardships for its members, and the governing structure of the Church does not permit its members to instigate any changes, even where a substantial majority support the reforms.

A good example is the Church's doctrine against birth control. Their current position is that birth control is sinful, except for "Natural Family Planning" with the rhythm method as its principal component. This means that using the pill, condoms, IUD's, vasectomies, tubal ligations, and even *coitus interruptus* is sinful in the eyes of the Church. Their justification for this rule is that God forbids sexual intercourse in all cases, except by a married couple for the purpose of conceiving a child. According to the Church, sex for any other purpose, such as for pleasure, is wrong and a sin against God.

Although the leaders of the Church would deny it, the main reason the Church prohibits most forms of birth control is that it wants to increase its membership base. They know that the best way to gain new members is to encourage Catholic couples to have as many children as possible, who will all grow up to be practicing Catholics. To that end, the Church leaders have decided that sex for the purpose of making babies is all right, but all other sex is sinful.

How can the Church condone the rhythm method while banning all other types of birth control? This rule makes no sense to me.

The Church leaders would have preferred to outlaw all forms of birth control, but they realized it was necessary to leave an opportunity for its members to space out their children and put a cap on the size of their families for financial and health reasons. So they decided to allow the rhythm method (which has a significant failure rate) and ban all other forms of birth control on the basis that the rhythm method is natural, and all the other methods are artificial. As a result, the Church still prohibits the most effective methods of birth control, but it has allowed its members one small hope to limit the number of babies they conceive. All of this is in keeping with the Church's goal of generating the greatest number of new Catholic members.

I do not understand how the Church can justify its position that using the pill or a condom is sinful, but the rhythm method is okay. Each method is intended to prevent conception.

As you have already noticed from your Catholic upbringing, the Catholic Church is not always logical or consistent with its policies. In fact, they often do not even attempt to justify some of their rules since they ultimately hide behind their assertion that the Pope is infallible, and everyone must obey his dictates (which really come from God) even if they are arbitrary or illogical. After all, according to the Church, humans should not try to understand the purpose for God's rules; He has good reasons for His rules, and they should be obeyed without question.

The distinction they have seized upon, that most forms of birth control are artificial, is a distinction without any meaningful difference. In fact, there is nothing natural about the rhythm method. In order for it to work, the woman must carefully monitor and record the timing of her menstrual cycle over a period of months and then count the days in her cycle to

determine which days she would not likely become pregnant. This whole process involves a close monitoring of her menstrual cycle and the ability to count days on a calendar. This method is not common in nature since it only works for humans who have the ability to create calendars and count days. Early humans who could not count and who did not have calendars were not able to use this method.

I have read several news articles about the widespread use of birth control by Catholics in the United States. A number of polls have indicated that a substantial majority of Catholics frequently use the pill or condoms and, despite the Church's position that such methods of birth control are sinful, they still believe they are good Catholics.

The Church does stubbornly cling to this ban on birth control even in light of strong opposition from its members. It is all part of the dictatorship of the Church; they insist that their members follow the dictates of the Pope even if they seem to be out of sync with modern civilization.

This brings to mind a couple of other rules that seem outdated and without any logical basis: the celibacy requirement for priests and the prohibition on women priests. When I was a teenager, the Church was already suffering from a shortage of priests, and it seems things have only gotten worse since then. It does not require a great leap of imagination to conclude that more men would apply for the job if priests could marry and have families. Moreover, if the Church allowed women to be priests, the potential pool of available candidates would double. The Church tries to justify these rules with faulty logic:

93

because Jesus was a man and he selected only men to be his apostles, they claim this means Jesus intended only men to be priests, and since Jesus never married and lived a celibate life (at least according to Church doctrine), all priests should live the same way so they can be "married" to the Church. The requirement for celibacy, which the Church has not applied consistently over its history, serves to confirm their underlying belief that sexual intercourse is impure, and their priests cannot attain the desired state of holiness if they engage in sexual activities. By implication, they are suggesting that married clergy in other religions are inferior to Catholic priests because they will be distracted by sex and family commitments.

One can easily conclude that their justification for not ordaining women priests is nothing but a convenient response that ignores the realities of our societies today. It strikes me that the leaders of the Church are an "old boys club" who prefer to maintain things the way they are, and they are not inclined to share their power with women. After all, if they allowed women to become priests, eventually there would be female bishops and cardinals and, ultimately, a female Pope.

Many Catholics today would share your view. The Church conveniently ignores the fact that Jesus lived on Earth at a time when most societies were patriarchal, and women could not assume prominent roles. You can imagine how difficult it would have been for Jesus to gather all of his followers and spread his message to the people if he had chosen to be born as a woman or if he had selected women as his apostles. However, in the developed countries of the world today, most people consider women equal to

men in every respect, and such societies would completely accept and respect women priests.

I have often wondered if the celibacy requirement for priests is one of the underlying causes of the sexual abuse of children by priests, numerous examples of which have come to light over the last few years. I believe sex is a very natural part of human existence, and it is unnatural and unhealthy for a person, especially a male, to abstain from having sex for long periods. It is not a long stretch to conclude that many of the cases of sex abuse by priests arose from their inability to obtain sexual release in the normal fashion by having sexual intercourse with a spouse.

You are not the only person who has made this connection although most people keep it to themselves. I agree that long periods of abstinence from sex can result in deviant behavior since it is natural for humans to engage in sexual intercourse on a regular basis.

It is unfortunate for the victims of such sexual abuse that the Church did not connect these dots years ago and abolish their celibacy policy for priests. It is even more unfortunate that this policy is still in effect today.

Enough said on that topic. I would like to ask you about two other hot-button issues for Catholics these days: abortion and homosexuality. As you know, the Church opposes abortion and considers homosexual acts to be contrary to natural law and sinful. Do you agree with the Church?

No, on both counts. The Church is very misguided on the abortion issue mainly because they do not understand the interaction between Souls and the human form. Souls do not occupy babies until the birth process has begun. Until then, the unborn baby is only a body and mind without a Soul. Humans must have Souls to survive, and they will perish without one. When a woman has an abortion, she is removing a human shell from her body since it has not yet been joined with a Soul. In most cases, abortions occur when the Soul who had planned to occupy the baby has changed its mind, or the Soul of the mother has changed its Life Plan, and it no longer wants to have the baby. In both situations, the two Souls will discuss the alternatives, and the abortion will not happen unless they both agree.

Homosexuality is not contrary to natural law, and it is not sinful or offensive to God. As I have said before, God does not make rules for humans to follow and has no desire to restrict or prohibit homosexual activities or anything else humans might do. The Church's ban on homosexual activities is consistent with their position that all sexual activities are sinful, except intercourse between a husband and wife for the purpose of conceiving a child. Since sex between homosexuals cannot result in conception, the Church considers these activities (along with most heterosexual activities) to be sinful.

So far, Albert, we have been focusing on the rules and beliefs of the Catholic Church and its use of guilt and fear to control its members. What about all the other religions in the world?

Surely the Catholic Church is not the only religion that uses these tools to manipulate its members.

Throughout the history of mankind, most organized religions have used guilt and fear to control their members and empower their leaders mainly by convincing the people that their holy men were following God's orders and anyone who ignored their dictates was offending God.

Many rules of organized religions deal with when, where, and how their members must worship God and obey His rules. For the most part, the observance or breach of these rules does not have any noticeable effect on society, positive or negative. For example, the prohibition on eating pork by several religions does not cause any harm (or any good, for that matter) to their members or society as a whole, and thus it is relatively innocuous. Likewise, the obligation to attend a religious service on a Saturday or Sunday is neutral to anyone who does not belong to that religion.

However, when holy men use religion to achieve their earthly desires, they often adversely affect society as a whole. Human history has numerous examples of holy men of different religions persuading their members to torture and kill other people in order to fulfill God's wishes. Numerous unthinkable acts have been committed at the behest of holy men who claimed to be following God's orders even though their real purpose was to further their own agendas and enhance their power.

By invoking the name of God, holy men have been able to convince others to sacrifice virgins, torture and kill infidels, burn heretics at the stake, and destroy villages full of women and children as part of a crusade to free the holy land. In more recent times, they have persuaded their followers to fly airplanes into office towers and strap bombs to their bodies to blow up innocent people. And these are only a few examples of the atrocities caused by organized religion and their holy men.

While it should not be surprising to you that holy men have often used God as a tool to wield power and achieve their goals, you may find it troubling that they have been so successful at finding gullible men to blindly follow their orders and cause so much harm. Somehow, most of these foot soldiers have been able to abdicate all of their moral principals in order to commit these horrible deeds, merely because a holy man tells them it is God's wish for them to do so.

I have often wondered about that myself. If God, who is all-powerful, really wanted a group of people or a country destroyed, why would He not use a lightning bolt to finish the job quickly and efficiently? Why does He need to enlist the crude efforts of men to carry out His wishes? And since God is the Supreme Being who hands out punishment in the hereafter, why does He not wait until these bad people die and then send them all to hell?

I think you know the answer to your question. As I have told you, God never interferes in human affairs, and He certainly does not ever tell holy men or anyone else that He wants certain people punished or destroyed because they have offended Him. God does not make rules for humans to follow, and there is nothing humans can do to offend Him. People follow the directions of these holy men because they have been duped into believing the holy men speak for God. And if God wants these atrocities committed, how can it be wrong to carry out His wishes?

I do not understand how this ploy has been able to fool all of these people. Did they not pause, even for a moment, to think about what these holy men were asking them to do? Could they not see the possibility that maybe these holy men were speaking for themselves and that God had nothing to do with it?

There are many people on your world who prefer to follow the easy path and not rock the boat. For them, it takes too much time and effort to analyze things for themselves, and they are content to go with the flow and follow the dictates of their holy men.

Are you not asking people to accept what you have been telling me at face value and reject what their holy men have been preaching? Why should they believe you? How can a person know for sure you are right, and their holy men are wrong?

No one should accept what I have told you without a careful and thoughtful examination of my truths in comparison to the beliefs preached by their holy men. You must examine these conflicting beliefs carefully, toss them around in your mind, and discuss them with your family and friends. Hold them up to the sun and look for any gaping holes. Shut out all the noise in your life and listen to your inner voice. Then embrace the belief that sits comfortably in your mind and feels right in your heart.

How do you know anyone will believe you?

I do not know if anyone will accept the things I have been telling you. I can only ask you to give them my message, and it is up to them to deal with it. Some people will believe what I have said, and others will dismiss it as nonsense. Eventually, over time, more and more people will come to accept what I have said, and humans will gradually move up the ladder to a higher level of consciousness.

Chapter Six

Sex Taboos

A few days after my first conversation with David, I saw him again at the gym. This time he invited me for coffee after the workout, and I could sense that he was troubled. He told me he had been thinking about the letter from the bishops warning married couples to be chaste in their sexual activities, and it brought back memories of all the sex taboos he had to live with in his early days.

"I grew up in an era when most adults thought sex was shameful and something that was never discussed at home or in polite company," David began. "Sex was a deep, dark secret that children were not supposed to know about until they were teenagers and then only for the purpose of warning them about unplanned pregnancies. In religion classes the priests and nuns never talked openly about sex, and they would use silly euphemisms to tell us that all thoughts, words, or actions relating to sex were sinful and offensive to God. They warned us that our conduct with the opposite sex had to be 'chaste,' and we should never do anything to make us 'impure' in the eyes of God. These sessions were not really sex education, as we know it today, since they did not give us any information about the male and female reproductive organs or any details

101

on sexual intercourse and conception. In a roundabout way, they did manage to convey their message that passionate kissing, petting, masturbation, sexual fantasies, and sexual intercourse, to name a few of the 'dirty' deeds on their list, were all grave sins and forbidden by God. Their list of sins was so long that it would have been nearly impossible for the average teenager to avoid sinning every day unless he was in a coma."

"This belief that everything relating to sex was taboo (except intercourse between spouses to conceive babies) became ingrained in the teenagers in our parish," he continued. "I can remember a date I had once with a girl from our parish. As I drove her home that evening, I mentioned a rumor I had heard about two of our classmates being caught having sex in the back seat of a car. She immediately launched into a tirade against sex, proclaiming that it was dirty and disgusting and that anyone who had sexual intercourse was a pig. When I reminded her that her parents had engaged in sexual intercourse or she would not have been born, she paused for a moment and then declared that her parents were pigs, just like everyone else. I was surprised at her vehemence, and I concluded that the Church would be pleased to know that their guilt and fear tactics about sex were working so well. I had no more dates with this young lady, and I found out years later that she eventually got married and had three children. I have often wondered if this meant she had changed her views on sex or if she had merely tolerated limited and joyless sex with her husband in order to conceive her children, all the while wondering if she was being impure."

"My experience with the Church was similar to yours," I conceded, "and I have often wondered since then why the Church had a multitude of rules about sex. And it was not only Catholics who had hang-ups about sex; all of my Protestant friends were in the same boat. It seemed that all adults in those days had similar views on sex, regardless of their religion. I can understand the reason for some of these rules, like no sex before marriage to avoid unwanted pregnancies, but I do not understand why they had rules that did nothing to protect individuals or society."

David frowned and then tried to answer my question. "As far as I can tell, sex taboos and rules restricting sex have been around in one form or another for centuries. In addition to Catholics, there have been many religions and secular societies throughout history with rules governing sexual conduct. A few of these rules were created to preserve peace and harmony in society. Their leaders recognized that humans were not naturally monogamous creatures, and it was necessary to establish rules to enforce this principle, along with harsh sanctions for breaching them. They knew that without rules to enforce monogamy and prohibit adultery, some men would have numerous sex partners while others might have none, thereby sowing the seeds for jealousy, anger, and violence. They also understood that a lifelong monogamous union of one man and one woman was the most stable and nurturing environment to raise children, and sexual intercourse outside of this relationship could result in unwanted and uncared for babies. As a result, these leaders decreed that sex with anyone who was not your spouse was unlawful and offensive to God. Given the development stage of their societies when these rules were established, it is understandable that they believed they were acting in the best interests of their members and society as a whole."

"The rationale for such rules does not always hold true in our modern society," he noted. "The widespread use of birth control makes it easier for people to have sex without the fear of an unwanted pregnancy, and many societies no longer consider fornication or children born out of wedlock to be shameful. In this respect, organized religions today are often lagging behind the mores of their members by clinging to rules that no longer have any relevance."

"I can understand the genesis of the monogamy and fornication rules," I countered, "but I have difficulty with all the rules that do not have any effect on society, positive or negative. Some religions still forbid married couples to engage in sexual activities unless it is to conceive a child although I find it difficult to understand how foreplay or intercourse with contraceptives can be bad for the couple or anyone else. Many religions consider masturbation, sexual fantasies, and sexual activities between homosexuals to be sinful even though none of these activities has any negative impact on the people involved or on society generally. Where did these rules come from and why are they still around?"

"I have thought about this a lot over the years," David continued, "and I have not been able to discover any rationale for these rules. Several critics have suggested that these rules originated with religious leaders who felt that sex was dirty, shameful, and offensive to God (except for making babies). The reasons for this attitude have never been readily apparent, and none has been offered by the men who proclaimed them other than the standard declaration that they were echoing God's view of sexual activities."

"Others have surmised that these rules originated from a general belief held by various holy men that pleasure of any kind, including pleasure from sex, is inherently bad as it weakens a person's resolve to obey God's rules. Still others have concluded that religious leaders strive to keep the list of sinful activities, including those relating to sex, as long as possible to ensure their members will be in a perpetual state of guilt, forcing them to attend church service regularly to seek salvation. There are even a few cynical Catholics I know who believe that these rules arose from the fact that Catholic clergy are not allowed to enjoy the pleasures of sex, so they passed these rules to ensure that no one else could enjoy sex either."

"Regardless of how these rules originated, most have been passed down through the centuries without anyone giving them a critical review. This is why, even today, societies and religions still have myriad rules that regulate sexual conduct. In recent times, there has been a change in attitude about sex although most of the taboos remain. For the most part, young people (and many older people) today do not share these views, and they are often perplexed when they try to understand where these rules came from and what evil they were designed to prevent."

I could tell that David was passionate about this topic, so I let him continue. "And this brings us back to the news item we discussed last week about the letter from the bishops. Do they really think they can convince everyone that God has a view on what is 'proper' sex for a married couple? Young people in our society (and from various religions) have no reluctance about living together out of wedlock, a practice that most adults of our generation have accepted even though it would have been scandalous to do so when we were young. Given this more liberal attitude on sexual relationships, it is hard to believe that these bishops feel the need to regulate the sex practices of married couples. In my opinion, this contributes to the Church's lack of credibility and it leaves them open to ridicule and scorn," he concluded.

"I think a majority of people today (regardless of their religion) would agree that all religions risk more and more attrition unless they can get their heads out of the Middle Ages and make an effort to become more relevant in today's society, especially when it concerns sex," I ventured.

David nodded his head as he rose to leave the room. "Most people, young and old, have already concluded that organized religions have too many meaningless rules and no credible answers to life's important questions, which is why church attendance has been declining for several decades. And I don't expect this is going to change any time soon," he said, as he headed out the door.

Although I knew David had hit the nail on the head with his points about religion and sex, I decided to ask Albert for his view on this topic.

When we discussed the rules of the Catholic Church, Albert, we touched briefly on the Church's attitude toward sex. Many of their rules try to restrict sexual activity even to the extent of prohibiting thoughts about sex, and most other organized religions have similar rules governing sexual activity. Are they right when they claim that their rules come from God? What does God really think about sex?

Sexual intercourse is a very natural and integral part of being a human. God created humans with sex organs and a strong sex drive, and He expected that they would engage in sexual activities on a regular basis. God designed sex to be pleasurable to encourage the practice, and it is not inherently wrong to enjoy sex. Sexual intercourse is as natural to humans as eating, drinking, and breathing. Sex between two consenting adults can be one of the most enjoyable and rewarding of all human activities. It can serve as the ultimate expression of love between two people, and it helps to complete and strengthen the bond between them. Furthermore, sexual intercourse is the way humans procreate, and it is a necessary component for the continuation of human life on Earth.

As I have mentioned before, God does not prescribe rules for humans to follow. God does not prohibit sex or restrict its use just as He does not prohibit or restrict any other human activities. God created humans with sex organs and a strong sex drive by design, not by accident, and He does not regard any sexual activities between consenting adults (or any solo activities) to be offensive or unnatural. If God did not want humans to have sex, He would have designed them differently. Religious leaders have always invoked the name of God to provide validity for their

rules, and the rules relating to sex are no exception. As we have discussed before, just because a holy man says a rule comes from God does not make it so.

This makes good sense to me. I have often wondered why God in His infinite wisdom would create humans with sex organs and raging hormones and then make rules to restrict sexual activity with the expectation that men and women would be able to control their natural desires. If parents did not want their four-year-old child to eat candy, they would not dream of leaving him alone in a room full of candy with the hope that he would be able to resist the temptation.

It is difficult to find flaws in your logic; however, you are not the person who gets to make or change the rules on sex. All you can do is inform others about our conversations and hope for the best.

Chapter Seven

Spirit Communication

Even though sex and religion are fascinating topics, Albert, I would like to move on and ask about your role as one of my Spirit Guides.

Spirit Guides are Souls on the Spirit Side who act as guides and coaches for Souls on Earth. Every person has several Spirit Guides at any given time although they will change during the course of a lifetime in order to better suit the person's needs. Most Spirit Guides have lived on Earth themselves, so they can appreciate what you are going through and the difficulties you will endure. Most often, your Spirit Guides are part of your spirit group, and they have lived in a close relationship with you in past lives. It is likely you have been one of their Spirit Guides in a previous life, or you will be for one of their future lives.

The main duty of your Spirit Guides is to give you guidance when you come to a fork in the road and have to make a decision. At these junctures, your Spirit Guides will send you messages to encourage you to take the right path—the path intended in your Life Plan—but you do not always hear or understand their messages because your mind is too cluttered with other thoughts. Often they send their messages in the form of an intuitive thought or feeling that suddenly pops into your head, and sometimes they are embedded in one of your dreams. At other times, you might receive guidance in the form of verbal statements made by other people (who are prompted by their Spirit Guides) or through the occurrence of "coincidental" events in your life. These messages are easy to miss unless you watch for them and take the time to decipher their meaning.

Whenever you get an intuitive thought or feeling (like a whisper in your mind), make sure you pause, listen carefully, and try to understand what it is trying to tell you. Most often, it is a message from your Soul and, at important junctures in your life, from your Spirit Guides as well. Frequently, your mind will ignore the whisper or rationalize a different course of action, but you must resist these tendencies and be more vigilant at following the guidance in these messages.

As an example, try to remember that day in January years ago when your mother turned sixty. You arrived at your office that morning in your usual rush and quickly scanned your meeting schedule and all the phone messages piled up on your desk. Then you noticed a note you had scribbled on your to-do list to phone your mother to wish her a happy birthday. The first feeling you got was an urge to make the call immediately before things got too hectic. Unfortunately, your mind kicked into gear, and you began to rationalize. You had so many phone calls to return and letters to read that it would be better to do these things first. Moreover, if you called your mother later in the day, you would have more time to chat.

Your initial feelings were coming from your Soul, but your mind came up with reasons to dismiss these feelings and ignore the message. As you know, your mind won this dispute, and you decided to make the call later. As you rushed through another busy day, you managed to forget about the call, and you did not remember to do it after you got home from work. You were the only one of your mother's five children who did not phone or pay her a visit on her special birthday.

I vaguely recall this, and I am embarrassed to be reminded about it now. I did remember to call Mom a couple of days later, but I know it was not the same as doing it on her birthday. I had no excuse for missing that call.

Your neglect was hurtful, but your mother was a very understanding person, and she knew your lapse was not intentional. Your mother is over here now, and she and your father are once again enjoying the love and happiness of the Spirit Side. They both continue to keep a watchful eye on their children, grandchildren, and great grandchildren, frequently sending positive and loving thoughts to their loved ones back on Earth.

They look forward to giving everyone a warm hug when they cross over to the Spirit Side.

Another example of the tug-of-war between your Soul and your mind was that Saturday afternoon when your three-year-old son asked you to read to him just as you were heading out the door to run a few errands. Your first impulse—which came from your Soul—was to sit down with your child and read from his *Dr. Seuss* book. But your second thought—coming from your mind—was to continue out the door since you had so many things to do and so little time to do them. Furthermore, your mind rationalized that you had spent a whole hour reading to him the night before, and surely that was good enough. Once again your mind won, and you walked out the door, leaving your disappointed child standing there clutching his book.

That hurts, Albert. I do recall this event although I did not realize at the time that my initial feelings—which I should have followed—were coming from my Soul, and I made the mistake of listening to my mind instead.

It is a mistake humans make all too often. Once you understand that such feelings are coming from your Soul and sometimes from your Spirit Guides, you will learn to listen carefully and become better at recognizing and *ignoring* the rationalizations that come from your mind.

What happened with my son after I ran out on him?

As usual, your wife saved the day. She scooped up little Blake, hugged him tenderly, and dried his tears. She cuddled with him on the sofa, reading from his book until he fell asleep for his nap. Even though your wife had more things to do that day than you did, she was not dismayed with this interruption to her schedule—she had listened to her Soul, and she knew that it was important to spend this time with your son. Your wife is a very intuitive person, and she is better at following guidance from her Soul than most people. You could do well by following her example.

I know what you mean. My wife has been the pillar of our family since day one—nurturing our sons from infancy to adulthood and providing loving comfort to me whenever my ship sailed into stormy waters (which seemed to happen quite often). Her advice to me during the low points in my life often embodied wisdom that seemed to come from a higher source. It is clear to me now that she was tuning in to the spirits.

You're are fortunate to have Cathy as your partner since you have spent most of your life rushing to meet your goals, blindly following the desires of your mind, and ignoring the guidance we have been sending you. And all too often, you have failed to listen to your wife (who could hear our messages) as she tried her best to nudge you in the right direction.

It seems that most of my life has been a blur. I have always felt that time was of the essence, and I had to hurry to achieve my goals as quickly as possible. After reaching each goal, I would continue to race toward the new goals I would set for myself. I can see now how I let my mind rule my life and that I always pushed my feelings away. I believed that listening to my feelings was a sign of weakness, and I prided myself on squelching them whenever possible.

I am wondering now, Albert, what you were doing when all this was happening. I thought you were supposed to help me when I needed direction.

There is an old saying on your planet: "If you want to teach something new to a mule, you first have to hit him over the head with a two-by-four to get his attention." In your case, we have nearly exhausted our supply of two-by-fours trying to get your attention. God knows we have tried everything in the book to get you to listen, but you were always so hell-bent on advancing your career that it was like talking to a post. Your team over here had trouble understanding why you were always racing down the track since you obviously did not even know where the finish line was—or what you would do if you ever reached it. That is why we decided to be more forceful, and I appeared in your life as the homeless man to get your attention.

Thank you for being persistent. I can now see all the mistakes I have made in my life by shutting out my feelings and the people who loved me. What can I do now to make amends?

You cannot change what has already happened in your life—it is water under the bridge. As to the future, however, you can choose now to live the rest of your life differently by listening to your feelings. If you can do this and put the rationalizations of your mind on the back burner, you will make us and all the people on Earth who are close to you very happy, and you will enjoy your life like never before.

We know this will not be easy for you, but you must begin with small, easy steps. So the next time your little dog prances up to you with a toy in her mouth, will you ignore her and keep on writing, or will you pause for a few moments to give her a little attention?

I will try to remember what you have said and give back to her the unconditional love she gives me every day.

Hallelujah!

Thanks, but that was easy to answer, even for me. I am more concerned about missing the subtle messages coming from my Soul and my Spirit Guides. How can I hone my listening skills?

Practicing meditation will help you hear these messages as it will calm your mind and clear out all of the thoughts you usually have swirling around in your mind. There is a long history of religious and spiritual men and women using meditation as a means to

115

connect with their "higher selves" and the universe. Meditation can help you open the channels of communication with your Soul and Spirit Guides so that you will be able to hear and understand more of the messages you receive every day from the Spirit Side. As an added benefit, meditation can relieve your stress and help you face your day-to-day struggles with a more serene outlook.

What is the best way for me to learn how to meditate? Can you recommend a method or learning process?

Humans have developed various methods of meditation, any one of which can work for you. There are dozens of books on this subject, and you can choose from many different courses designed to teach you how to meditate. You should use the method that feels right to you, and then practice and practice until you can achieve the mindfulness necessary for you to understand the desires of your Soul and hear the messages from your Spirit Guides.

This seems like a lot of work. It is easier for me to speak to you as we are doing right now. Will you always be able to communicate with me through telepathy?

I have the capability to do so; however, I will not use this method to replace the normal flow of messages sent to you by your Soul and other Spirit Guides. I am using this direct telepathic communication to make it easier for you to ask your questions and hear the answers so you can pass this information on to others.

I will not use this method to allow you to find out what is in your Life Plan or to give you the right answers on decisions you will have to make in the future. If I did so, everything would be too easy for you, and it would be more difficult for you to reach the goals you had established for your current life. For the normal course messages we want you to have, you will have to rely on your ability to discern them as they come, like everyone else.

Is it possible for other Souls on the Spirit Side, such as loved ones who have already passed on, to communicate with people on Earth?

It is possible although it happens infrequently. Many people have enjoyed contacts with loved ones that have recently crossed over, but often they are one-time events that do not recur on a regular basis.

I asked you this question because of what happened to me a couple years ago. I was reading the newspaper on a Sunday morning when the phone rang. It was my sister-in-law, Paulette, who told me that my brother, Brian, had stopped breathing earlier that morning. She told me that the paramedic team who answered the 9-1-1 call was able to restore his breathing and transport him to the hospital where he was on life support but not conscious. She said they did not know how long he had been "dead" before the paramedics arrived, and there could be irreversible brain damage, an issue she would discuss with his doctors after they had finished their examination.

Following this call, I went to my bedroom to be alone as I thought about my brother, crossing my fingers that everything would turn out for the best. After an hour or so, I was startled out of my reverie when the lights suddenly went out, and our neighbor's security system began sounding its siren, which it always did when the power failed. I glanced at my watch to note the time, but within ten seconds, the lights flickered back on. Twenty-five minutes later, Paulette called to say that my brother had died peacefully at 1:15 pm, which was the same time as our short power failure. I sensed immediately that Brian had caused our power outage to say farewell and to let me know he was safe and sound on the Spirit Side.

As another example, my wife believes she had contact with her deceased mother not long after she had passed away from terminal cancer. It happened when our son, Colin, was singing in the vocal ensemble for his high school. One day early in the school year, the group's teacher proudly announced they (along with several other high school groups from North America) had received an invitation to perform the next April at a concert in Carnegie Hall, New York. This was all very exciting until we found out the school board would not permit this trip to New York because all the field trips allocated to this school for the current year had already been booked by other groups, and they were not prepared to make an exception.

The group's parents were very upset at this decision. With my wife as one of the leaders, they formed a committee to prepare an appeal to the school board. Cathy and the other parents worked very hard on this project, and despite all the obstacles they had to overcome along the way, they managed to convince the board to reverse its earlier decision and allow the vocal ensemble to go to Carnegie Hall. After the fact, Cathy confided to me that at one point during the process, she had become so discouraged that she was ready to throw in the towel. Then she felt the presence of her mother placing one hand on her shoulder and giving her loving encouragement to continue with the appeal. This contact with her mother inspired her to finish the appeal.

Can you tell me, Albert, if these contacts really came from the Spirit Side, or were they conjured up by our imaginations?

If you believe in your hearts that these contacts came from the Spirit Side, then they were for real, and you will cherish them for the rest of your lives. You should consider yourselves fortunate since not all people have the opportunity to enjoy such contacts with their deceased loved ones.

To finish answering your question, however, there are humans, often called psychics or mediums, who have the ability to communicate regularly with Souls on the Spirit Side. Many of them receive verbal thought messages from the spirits while others are shown images or symbols they have to interpret. Trance mediums will go into in a trance to allow a spirit to temporarily step into their bodies and use the medium's speech organs to speak to those present. Souls on the Spirit Side are often able to communicate with their loved ones through psychics and mediums. Most often, they want to reassure their loved ones they are alive and well on the Spirit Side despite their physical death on Earth.

Communication with Souls on the Spirit Side is similar to finding a music station on your radio. If you do not have the tuner set to a specific frequency, you will not hear the music. Psychics and mediums have the ability to dial in to the right frequency in order to listen to Souls on the Spirit Side while most humans only hear static.

If I learn to communicate with Souls on the Spirit Side or if I contact them through a psychic, can they tell me what lies ahead in my future?

For obvious reasons, Souls on the Spirit Side are restricted from giving you specific details about your future, such as the date and manner of your death or similar details about your family and friends. To a limited extent, however, they can help you understand the messages from your Soul and your Spirit Guides so you can align your future decisions and actions more closely with your Life Plan.

Does this mean the Spirits Guides will not give me a winning lottery ticket number?

Of course not, and I am surprised that you would even ask that question. Have you already forgotten my advice about not following the desires of your mind? Stay right where you are. I am going to see if I can find one more two-by-four.

Chapter Eight

Life on the Spirit Side

Can you tell me more, Albert, about who you are and what you do on the Spirit Side?

As I told you earlier, I am one of your Spirit Guides for your present incarnation. I have lived on your planet numerous times myself, and I agreed to be one of your Spirit Guides when you were preparing the Life Plan for your current life. You and I are members of the same spirit group, and we have enjoyed many lives together on Earth. In our most recent incarnation together, you were my father and we lived in rural Ireland in the nineteenth century. You were a potato farmer who struggled to feed and clothe your wife and four children. As I was your only son, I toiled in the fields beside you from an early age, but I did not resent the hard labor. I learned a lot from you in that life, most importantly that I should never give up pursuing my goals despite all the obstacles that might get in the way. Although you died from pneumonia when you were only 39, you did manage to eke out enough of a living from the land to allow your wife and children to survive.

In one of our earlier lives together in fifteenth century Britain, I was a minor lord and you were my manservant. I had a tragic fall from my horse when I was a young man, leaving me crippled and confined to my bed for the rest of that life. You provided me with loving care and attention until I died, and I loved you as a brother. We had daily conversations about the meaning of life, and we learned much from each other during our time together.

We have lived in dozens of countries and in various different relationships. Often you were my mother or father, and other times we were siblings. In a few incarnations we were spouses or friends. We have always enjoyed our adventures together even though this was often not apparent to us until after we had both returned to the Spirit Side.

How many lives have I had so far on this planet?

Several hundred. The exact number is not important for you to know at this time.

Does this mean that I am supposed to be wise?

Not necessarily. Sometimes old Souls are just slow learners.

I find this topic fascinating. Can you tell me more about my previous lives?

In one life in the fourteenth century in Italy (as it is now known), you were a monk who tended the monastery's vineyards and made delicious wine. You loved your job, and you were generous about sharing your wine with the people in the nearby villages. That was a jolly life for you—full of good food, great wine, and loyal companions.

In a more recent life in Scotland, you grew up in a small village with your identical twin brother (who is someone you know in your current life). Both of you were mischievous rascals, and you drove each other and your mother crazy with your antics.

You often chose the life of an explorer, and you frequently traveled into uncharted territories. On one occasion, you drowned in the Amazon River after falling off your raft during a violent storm.

This is all very intriguing. Please continue.

I could go on, but it would not serve any useful purpose for you at this time. You will be able to review all of your previous lives when you return to the Spirit Side. In the meantime, you should continue with your other questions so you can finish your book before you die of old age.

All right, we will leave the questions about my past lives for another time. Can you tell me why you decided to be one of my Spirit Guides? Do I have other Spirit Guides?

I freely chose to be one of your Spirit Guides because I believed I was well suited for this role in your current life. I did so with great joy as I love you very much. I know you love me as well, and you will likely be one of my Spirit Guides in a future incarnation.

All humans have several Spirit Guides at any given time, but the spirits who fill that role come and go as your life progresses to ensure that you always have the best team of coaches for each stage of your life. You currently have three Spirit Guides, including me. I am not able to give you any more details on your other Spirit Guides since this could compromise the events you have planned for your life.

Is it difficult to be a Spirit Guide? Does it occupy all of your time on the Spirit Side?

Being a Spirit Guide is a great joy and labor of love. Even though you do not always hear or follow my messages, I understand why this is so. I know that no matter what happens on Earth, neither you nor I can fail. It is like a mother watching her baby learning to walk. She watches her child take the first few tentative steps and fall down repeatedly; however, she is not anxious or impatient, as she knows her toddler will eventually learn to walk, and there is no need for this to happen quickly. Similarly, I know you will make many mistakes, and you will often stray off course, but ultimately you will end up back here on the Spirit Side, none the worse for the wear.

Souls who are Spirit Guides are not fully occupied in this role; they can be engaged in other activities at the same time.

What do you do on the Spirit Side when you are not watching over me?

I am always watching over you—I never abandon my post—although I continue with my other activities at the same time. Most Souls on the Spirit Side have "jobs" or projects they freely choose for themselves, but they don't have to do anything on the Spirit Side if that is their choice. Souls pursue various activities on the Spirit Side to increase their knowledge and evolve. Many Souls offer assistance to other Souls who are creating new Life Plans while others will help those Souls who have recently crossed over become reacquainted with the Spirit Side. None of these activities is difficult or what you would consider work on Earth. We do these things freely and with great love and joy.

Souls do not have appointments or schedules on the Spirit Side. Souls can choose where they want to be and what they want to do without any concern about how much time they spend at each activity since linear time as you know it does not exist on the Spirit Side. Even though humans consider a life span of eighty years to be a long time, it is only the "blink of an eye" on the Spirit Side. A Soul's incarnation on Earth does not result in a noticeable interruption of its activities on the Spirit Side since the time spent during a life on your planet is relatively insignificant.

125

The Spirit Side must be a delightful place. Is it necessary for Souls on the Spirit Side to eat or drink?

Souls on the Spirit Side do not need to eat, drink, or breathe. They do not need clothing, shelter, or a means of transportation. Anything a Soul wants, it can create instantly by *thought creation*. Even though they have no real need for them, Souls can create for themselves the things they enjoyed on Earth or wished they had been able to enjoy. A Soul can *thought create* a huge mansion on a lovely beach or a log cabin in the mountains and live there until it no longer desires to do so. If a Soul wants to go to another location, it can travel there instantly with *thought creation*, or it can create a red Ferrari and drive there. If a Soul loved dining out in fine restaurants during its last incarnation, it can *thought create* gourmet restaurants and dine at them as often as it likes even though Souls on the Spirit Side have no need to eat.

Do Souls engage in sex on the Spirit Side? Do they get married and have children?

Sexual activities in the Earth sense do not happen on the Spirit Side. Quite often, however, two Souls will choose to fuse their energies together for a few moments of sheer ecstasy. This is not for the purpose of procreation, since Souls on the Spirit Side do not have children, but merely for the intense pleasure derived from this temporary union. There are no spouses or committed relationships on the Spirit Side, and thus these interactions do not breach any

commitments or cause jealousy. These mergers between two Souls happen freely and openly, and they never have any effect on other Souls. Although Souls do not have families in the Earth sense, they do belong to spirit groups that are like large, extended families.

What about gender on the Spirit Side? Are there male and female Souls, and does this affect the gender they choose when they incarnate on Earth?

Souls do not have a specific gender on the Spirit Side. Souls will often choose to appear to other Souls in either the male or the female form, but this is a matter of personal preference for the Soul. Souls can incarnate as either gender and most Souls will choose both sexes over the course of their lifetimes in order to experience all facets of life as a human.

Are there sports and recreational activities on the Spirit Side? Do they have golf courses over there?

Anyone who wants to golf on the Spirit Side can do so whenever she chooses without reserving tee times. Souls can play on one of the courses created by other Souls, or a Soul can *thought create* its own course. In order to make it fun and challenging, Souls who golf do not use *thought creation* to influence the flight of the ball since shooting a hole-in-one on every hole would soon be boring.

Besides golf, every sporting and recreational activity humans enjoy on Earth is available on the Spirit Side. You can downhill ski, surf, snorkel, parasail, kayak, hike, and climb mountains, to name a few, as well as all of the indoor activities like bowling, squash, and billiards. You can watch theatrical plays, attend musical concerts, or enjoy sitting in the warm sunshine while cheering for your favorite baseball team. If you like, you can get together with friends for a chat over a beer.

If you want to expand your knowledge, you can attend lectures given by famous professors and experts, arrange for private tutoring sessions on any topic you wish, or read books or watch videos by yourself in one of our libraries.

There are no entrance fees or reservations required for any activity on the Spirit Side and never any waiting lines. If you get tired of the activities you remember from Earth, you can engage in all the different types of sports and recreation common on other planets, or you can invent new ones. There are no limits to the kinds of activities available to you, other than the limits of your own imagination.

What about hunting and fishing? Since these activities involve the killing of another creature, they would seem to be out of place on the Spirit Side.

These "sports" are available on the Spirit Side although the animals involved are just illusions created by the hunters with *thought creation*. Since Souls on the Spirit Side have no desire to injure or kill other creatures even if they are not for real, such

activities are rare; usually they are pursued by Souls who have recently crossed over from Earth and still retain their Earthly desires. Eventually these Souls lose interest in hunting and fishing and move on to other activities.

I am happy to learn I will have no trouble being active and challenged on the Spirit Side. When I was a young man, I remember that movies often depicted heaven as a place up in the sky where people would sit on fluffy white clouds and listen to angels play harps. While this seemed to be a nice alternative to getting up early every day to go to work, I wondered if a person might become bored in heaven if this was all there was to do.

Boredom only occurs on your planet. Because there are countless things to do on the Spirit Side and millions of stars and planets to explore, a Soul will never be able to see or do everything in the universe even with the eternal lifespan that all Souls enjoy. If a Soul desires contrast to the never-ending array of interesting, amusing, and challenging activities on the Spirit Side, it can incarnate on one of the planets in the denser planes, such as Earth, to get a dose of the harsh conditions and difficult challenges that go with such a life. A Soul who has just returned from a difficult incarnation will appreciate the ecstasy of the Spirit Side even more than before.

So when I return to the Spirit Side, I will not have to sit on a cloud and listen to harp music every day?

No, because I will make sure you get live in one of our "harp-free" zones over here. But you should reconsider your reluctance to sit on a cloud—they are really quite comfortable.

Please forgive me if I don't laugh aloud, Albert. I hope your humor will improve before I get back to the Spirit Side.

I will start working on that right away.

In the meantime, I have a few more questions about Souls and the Spirit Side. You mentioned before that Souls who incarnate on Earth are at different levels of evolution. Are Souls on the Spirit Side at different levels of advancement? Is there a hierarchy of Souls on the Spirit Side?

Souls on the Spirit Side exist on many different levels of advancement or evolution, based upon the knowledge and the wisdom they gained from previous incarnations. As I have said, Souls can acquire knowledge on the Spirit Side in various ways, including reading books, watching videos, attending lectures, participating in discussion groups, and enjoying private sessions with the Wise Ones. Souls also learn a great deal from their life reviews after each incarnation and from watching other Souls undertake their own life reviews. Souls can learn much by acting as a Spirit Guide for another Soul during one of its incarnations. Perhaps the best way

for Souls to learn is by exploring the universe—by traveling as spirits (without incarnating into physical bodies) to the stars and planets that exist in the denser planes of the universe. During these adventures, Souls can learn a lot about the universe, and this knowledge will help them choose the planet for their next incarnation.

Ultimately, most Souls will choose to incarnate on the denser planes to experience the things they need in order to complete the knowledge they have acquired as spirits. The wisdom so gained from their lives on the denser planes allows Souls to accelerate their rate of evolution. Since Souls do not progress at the same pace—some are more advanced than other Souls—but there is no hierarchy of Souls in the Earth sense. All Souls on the Spirit Side are equal, and the more advanced Souls are not considered superior to or better than the less advanced Souls. It is like schools on Earth where high school seniors are not regarded as better than kindergarten students—just more advanced in their formal education. All Souls continue to evolve—there are never any failures, and there are no timetables or deadlines to meet.

What is the purpose of evolution for a Soul? What happens when a Soul has advanced through all the levels? What is at the finish line?

Souls grow and evolve because that is the only direction they can go. Souls never go backwards; they always move onward and upward. Souls evolve in order to become more like God in every respect, which is a moving target because God is constantly changing. There is no end to the levels of advancement for a Soul and no finish line. The universe is infinitely vast with an infinite number of planes or dimensions that are always changing. Souls can never finish exploring and experiencing the universe since there is no end to the universe and its constant state of change. Every new experience in the universe provides Souls with the opportunity to continue to grow and evolve in a never-ending process.

You are telling me that my Soul is on a journey with no final destination, a trek with no end. I find it hard to wrap my mind around this concept. Can you explain this in a way that I can understand?

The journey of the Soul I have described is difficult for the human mind to comprehend fully. It is similar to a human trying to grasp the concepts of eternity and infinity, which cannot be understood completely due to the inherent limitations of the human mind on the Earth plane. It would be like a person who has been blind since birth trying to understand color when he hears other people talk about the grass being green or the rose bloom having a bright red hue. Do not become discouraged about this because you will once again understand the meaning and purpose of the journey of your Soul when you return to the Spirit Side.

I guess I have no choice except to wait until I am back on the Spirit Side in order to understand all of these esoteric concepts.

Do not be in a rush to get back here; you still have much to do in your life. You need to suck it up and enjoy the ride.

Chapter Nine

Many Lives, Many Places

So far, Albert, we have been talking about Souls incarnating into humans, but you mentioned that Souls could also incarnate on other planets. Does this mean there is life on other planets?

Did you really think God created all the stars in the universe so humans would have something pretty to look at every night? The universe has millions of stars with planets that support life in different forms. Souls on the Spirit Side can choose to incarnate into life forms on any of these planets.

Do any of these planets have intelligent life? Is there life out there that is more advanced than human life?

There is life in the universe that has intelligence similar to humans, and many such life forms have intellects that greatly surpass the human intellect and technology that is superior to what humans have developed so far.

Your perspective on life forms, however, is tainted by your human mindset. Humans believe intelligent life

must be similar to humans with the ability to think, reason, and develop technology. This is a very simplistic and somewhat arrogant viewpoint. Intelligent life in the universe comes in many forms, and some do not have any technology at all. Humans tend to believe that technological advancement is the only true measure of the status of a life form, but this view is too narrow. Souls on the Spirit Side can appreciate the bigger picture, and this provides them with opportunities to incarnate on planets with life forms that are quite different from humans.

Why haven't any of these advanced life forms contacted humans to make their presence known to us?

Many of these advanced civilizations have observed the Earth since it was formed, and several have traveled to your planet to interact with its life forms, including humans. They have chosen not to have open contact with humans so far because it would not be in the best interests of humans in their current stage of development or would serve no useful purpose from their perspective. There will be a time in Earth's future when humans will have open contact with these life forms.

So when I return to the Spirit Side after this life, I can choose to incarnate into a life form on another planet.

Yes you can, and your decision will be based on what you have experienced so far and what you need to experience next to advance your evolution. This might mean that you will choose to return to Earth for further incarnations, or you may decide to try life on a different planet instead.

As I mentioned before, Souls on the Spirit Side can travel throughout the universe as spirits in order to explore the planets that sustain life forms. During such adventures, Souls can secretly observe these life forms without causing any disruption to their normal pattern of life. The information gathered from such missions is very useful to a Soul when it is deciding which planet and life form it will choose for its next incarnation. The variety of choices available is almost unimaginable with each life form and each planet having its own unique set of circumstances and challenges. Since Souls are eternal and there are no timetables for their evolution, they have unlimited opportunities to experience life anywhere in the universe in every form they desire.

If Souls can incarnate into different life forms found on other planets in the universe, can they also incarnate into different life forms on Earth? Can Souls incarnate into animals?

Of course. Souls can incarnate into animals on Earth if they choose.

This possibility is troubling to me. Life as a human has more than enough difficult challenges, and I cannot quite imagine what it would be like to incarnate into a rabbit where every day you would be in constant danger of becoming a meal for a fox or an eagle. It must be a horrible existence.

Once again, you are viewing things from a human perspective. Rabbits do face many dangers, and their life spans are shorter than a typical human life span as a result. On the other hand, they live their lives on a day-to-day basis without worrying about becoming a predator's dinner since they are not capable of contemplating or anticipating future events. They also do not have to worry about what schools their children should attend, making mortgage payments, saving for retirement, or who to vote for in the next election.

Humans have the very arrogant belief that they live better lives than all other animals on your world. They conclude that having brains that allow them to think and reason and opposable thumbs that enable them to manipulate tools makes them superior in every sense to all other creatures. However, how can humans make the judgment that their lives are better than a dolphin's life until they have lived the life of a dolphin? Are humans better than dolphins because they can watch television and eat pizza?

Souls that contemplate incarnating into animals on Earth do not consider it to be horrible or terrifying, at least no more so than incarnating into a human. Every incarnation offers your Soul different opportunities, and you get to choose the challenges you want in any given life.

You should know, however, that most Souls that choose to incarnate as animals do so before they begin their human incarnations. Since most other animals live relatively simple lives compared to humans, Souls who are new to the Earth plane will often start out with a simpler life as an animal before moving on to more complex human lives although Souls can skip this step and begin their lives with human incarnations. It is rare for a Soul that has incarnated as a human to subsequently choose to incarnate as an animal since it would like a senior in high school deciding to attend first grade classes; there wouldn't be enough of a challenge to make it worthwhile. As you are now in human form, it is unlikely you will choose to incarnate as an animal in a future life.

Does this mean animals haves souls?

You need only look into the eyes of your little dog to find your answer. Animals also have Souls that cross over to the Spirit Side when they die.

If my dog dies before I do, will I see her again when I cross over?

Absolutely. She will be part of your welcoming party on the Spirit Side, eagerly awaiting your return.

I am happy to hear that. What you have said makes sense to me for dogs, cats, and other higher forms of animals, but what about lower forms of life, such as insects?

What you would term "lower" forms of life are all part of a universal life force created by God that connects all living things to everything else in the universe. On occasion, Souls will undertake a brief visitation in such animals as part of their Earthly adventures, but they do not ever occupy such animals from birth to death as they would with a human. Lower life forms have very simple lives, so a Soul can encounter everything there is to experience in such an animal in a very short time.

It has occurred to me that it must be especially difficult for animals to live without being able to anticipate future events. For example, our little dog, Abby, hates going to the vet or to the groomer. So when I lift her into my vehicle, she often trembles because she does not know if I am taking her to the groomer (which she hates) or to the beach (which she loves). Moreover, when she wakes up on the morning of her vet appointment, she does not know that this day will be different from the other days in her life until I carry her into the vet's office. At least I am aware of a few events in my future. I know I have a dental appointment next Thursday at 9:00 a.m., and on Saturday morning I leave for a vacation.

You might think you know some of the events that will happen in your future, however, nothing is certain on the Earth plane. You could die in a car accident on your way to the dentist, or you might keel over with a heart attack while on vacation. It is possible you have a malignant tumor growing in your brain right now, as we speak. There are many things that can happen to interfere with the events you plan in your life, and you cannot predict your future with any certainty.

I guess you are right although I never thought about it in that way. From your perspective on the Spirit Side, can you tell me what lies ahead in my future?

I can tell you that one day you will die, and your Soul will return to the Spirit Side; however, I cannot give you any more details since it would interfere with your Life Plan and the goals you have established for your current life. A big part of your adventure is dealing with the uncertainties of life and the challenge of being able to confront unexpected events, both good and bad, with a positive attitude while feeling only love and compassion for everyone around you.

I already knew what your answer would be, but it was worth a shot. If you change your mind, will you let me know?

I will, but don't hold your breath.

Chapter Ten

Karma

I was at the local supermarket recently to pick up a loaf of bread and a carton of milk. The store was very busy with long lines at every checkout. As I lined up at the end of one of the queues, a young woman pushing a full cart arrived at the same time, and I gallantly waved for her to go ahead of me. To my surprise, she shook her head and motioned for me to go ahead of her.

When she saw the puzzled look on my face, she said, "I need the karma."

As I waited in line, I kept thinking about what she had said. If she got karma credits for letting me go ahead of her, did I lose credits at the same time? Had I unwittingly allowed this person to gain easy karma credits at my expense?

The next day I went back to the supermarket with a plan. I picked up a couple of items and went to one of the checkout queues. I politely waved nine other shoppers, one at a time, to go ahead of me in the lineup. After finally reaching the till and paying for my groceries, I left the store wearing a wide grin. I had very cleverly gained positive karma from those people, and they did not even know it. Then I paused; if I could gain

143

positive karma so easily at the expense of those people, did I lose credits for stealing their karma?

That evening I researched the law of karma on the Internet. I discovered there are several different views about the nature of karma and how it affects everything in the universe. For many people, karma is the law of "cause and effect" that operates to ensure "you reap what you sow" and "what goes around comes around." For these people, karma is an immutable law of the universe like the law of gravity that governs all actions in the universe. In simple terms, if I punch a person in the nose, I have created a karmic "debt" that must be repaid later in this life or in another life in order to balance the books. I can repay this debt by receiving a similar negative action (e.g. somebody punches me in the nose), or I can rebalance the karma with a positive action directed toward another person. Under this regime, I would be compelled to continue incarnating on Earth until I had repaid the karmic debt I had accumulated from all of my previous lives.

There are also several religions that believe individuals' karmic balance at the end of one life determines who they will be in their next life. If they live good lives and do not create karmic debts, their next life will be better than their current lives. If they are bad in this life, their next life will be worse.

I wondered, "If this was how karma worked, how I could find out where I stood on the karmic scale. Was I in a positive or negative balance? Did all actions have the same karmic credits or debits, or were some actions worth more than other actions?" In fairness, I thought there should be a way for people to check their karmic balances on an ongoing basis. I wondered if I could buy a karma meter at Best Buy.

I decided to learn the truth about karma from Albert. As usual, Albert was there to answer my questions.

Albert, I have been struggling with the concept of karma, and I would like to know if karma exists and if it does exist, how does it fit into the grand scheme of things you have described. Several religions believe the law of karma determines the circumstances of individuals' next lives, based on what they do in their current lives. Others believe that karma is the law of "cause and effect" that operates to ensure all actions in the universe are balanced.

Neither of these views of karma is correct. The problem with the first view is that a Soul would not have a free hand in creating Life Plans for its lives since the laws of karma would dictate the particulars of each new life based on the Soul's past performance. The "cause and effect" view also would restrict a Soul's ability to create a Life Plan of its own choosing since karma would prescribe what must be included in order to balance all previous actions. As well, a Soul with a karmic debt would not be free to stop incarnating at any time since that Soul would be forced to continue with its lives until it had balanced its karma.

All Souls have the right to choose when and where to incarnate and to create their own Life Plans. Souls also have the right to stop incarnating on Earth

whenever they choose. These rights are not restricted in any way by God or karma. Karma is not an immutable law of the universe. Karma is a system for tracking the positive and negative actions of Souls during their incarnation. After each life, a Soul will note its karmic balance from all of its previous incarnations, and this will influence the Soul's selection of its next life and the events to be included in its Life Plan. Souls have a strong desire to balance their karma on Earth as part of their evolution, but they are never forced to do so. They always have the right to ignore a karmic debt if they so choose.

This makes sense to me and is consistent with what you have told me about the incarnation process and the evolution of the Soul. Since Souls have a strong desire to repay karmic debt even though they are not forced to do so, it means people should still strive to be good so they can improve their karmic score cards. Souls need positive karmic balances so they can feel comfortable about graduating from Earth plane.

You are right. People can create positive karma by treating everyone else with love, compassion, and forgiveness, and avoiding the temptation to react in a negative way to the pain other humans have inflicted on them. Positive acts often have a multiplier effect that can inspire others to be kind and compassionate as well. Unfortunately, negative acts can have the opposite result. Before you take any action in your life, always ask yourself what your Soul would want you to do in this situation, and then do your best to fulfill your Soul's desire. If you can do this, you will enjoy a much happier life, you will spread love and happiness to those around you, and you will help your Soul with its evolution.

I would like to learn more about how positive and negative actions affect a Soul's karmic scorecard. If I gain karma credits by letting another shopper go ahead of me in the checkout queue, does that person lose an equal number of credits? If so, do I lose any credits for trying to gain credits at another person's expense?

Karma is not a zero-sum game. In your example, you would gain karma credits for your generous deed, but the person on the receiving end would not lose any credits. There is no action you can take that will provide you with credits at the expense of another person. The sum total of all positive and negative actions of all Souls on Earth does not have to balance. There have been many periods during the history of humans when the collective karmic score of all Souls has been very negative. Humans have been making great progress in the quest to create more and more positive karma, and at some point in your future, the collective karma on Earth will be positive. This will be a momentous occasion for your planet, and everyone on the Spirit Side will give you a standing ovation.

No doubt the Earth will be a much happier place when we achieve that goal. Can you tell me, Albert, how karma credits are measured? Do some actions have a higher value than others? And who determines the relative karmic value of actions on Earth?

147

The relative karmic value of a Soul's actions is determined by the Soul when it returns to the Spirit Side after each incarnation. During its life review, when it is in a much better position to understand how its good and bad deeds affected others, each Soul assigns a value to its actions as part of its overall assessment of its previous life. Some actions carry more weight than others. Dropping some coins into the hat of a homeless person generates positive karma, but spending three hours on a Saturday serving meals in a soup kitchen is even more positive. Karmic valuation is an art, not a science, and each Soul makes its own good faith determination of its karmic score after each life on Earth.

Chapter Eleven

The Illusion of Time

Now that you have explained how karma works, Albert, do you have time to answer a few more questions that have popped into my mind after reflecting on our conversations?

I have as much time as you need since linear time as you know it on Earth does not exist on the Spirit Side.

I recall that you mentioned this before about time on the Spirit Side, but I must admit I do not understand this concept. Can you explain it to me?

This is a very difficult concept for humans to understand since it is so foreign to what they observe all around them every day. The perceived interval between the start and finish of events is called time, which can be measured by clocks. Since there is no *thought creation* on Earth (at least not in the way it operates on the Spirit Side), events do not happen instantly. If you are playing catch with your son, at one point the ball is in your hand, and later after you have tossed the ball toward your son, the ball is in his glove. The interval between the ball starting out in

your hand and then ending up in your son's glove is called time, which can be measured in seconds. On the Spirit Side, the ball would start out in your hand and then appear instantly in your son's glove through *thought creation*. There would be no discernible interval in between these events as they both would happen concurrently.

Thought creation would be a wonderful tool for humans to use. It would make life so much easier. Why can't we use thought creation here?

What you have on Earth is like *thought creation* in slow motion. All actions and creations in the universe begin with a thought. On your planet if you think you would like to eat an apple, you must take several steps to achieve that goal. You put on your jacket, find your car keys, and drive to the supermarket. After finding a parking spot, you enter the store, pick out an apple, and pay for it at the till. Then you get back into your car and drive home. You will then be back where you started, except now you have an apple in your hand. This whole process from your first thought that you wanted an apple until you had one in hand might take fifteen or twenty minutes with many intermediate thoughts and actions. On the Spirit Side, if you want an apple it will appear in your hand instantly through *thought creation*.

The reason you do not have *thought creation* on Earth is to ensure that everything happens very slowly (relative to the Spirit Side) to give Souls a chance to understand all the events in their lives and how their actions affect others. The interval between the beginning and the end of an event provides Souls the opportunity to reflect on the outcome of their actions before the next event occurs.

If you are watching a football game on television, everything moves so quickly with the live action that you will often miss many of things that happen on the field. It is only when you watch the slow-motion replay of the touchdown pass that you notice the great block the right tackle threw on the linebacker and the head fake the wide receiver used to get in the clear.

The illusion of linear time on the Earth plane allows Souls to view events in "slow-motion"; it is a learning tool to help Souls appreciate the effect of their decisions and actions and give them a better understanding of their experiences on your planet.

Are there not certain events on the Spirit Side, like the rising and setting of the sun, that occur before or after other events? Would the difference not be considered an interval of time?

On the Spirit Side, the sun does not rise or set as you know it. Souls on the Spirit Side can choose to be in daylight or darkness whenever they want, and not everyone has to follow the same pattern. If the transition from daylight to darkness and back to daylight again occurs, it is instantaneous; there is no noticeable interval between the two. Similarly, everything else on the Spirit Side occurs

151

instantaneously and concurrently, so there are never intervals between events that can be noticed or measured.

This means that on the Spirit Side there is no past or future as you understand it. When you are holding the ball and ready to throw it, you can anticipate that it will travel through the air and land in your son's glove. This to you is the future. After you have thrown the ball to your son, your previous act of holding the ball in your hand is something that is now in the past. However, since all events on the Spirit Side happen concurrently, everything that has happened in the "past" or that will happen in the "future" is all happening now in the present.

To help you understand, let me give you an example (which is an oversimplification of what happens on the Spirit Side) using images that are familiar to you. Imagine you are standing in the middle of a football field, facing the home team bench. You notice the home team cheerleaders leading a cheer on the sidelines. At the same time, behind you the cheerleaders for the visiting team are also doing their routine. You can see the home team cheerleaders because you are facing them, but you cannot see the other cheerleaders because they are behind you. If you turn around 180 degrees, you will now see the visiting team cheerleaders, and the home team cheerleaders will no longer be visible. To you, the cheer from the home team's cheerleaders happened first, followed by the routine of the visiting team's cheerleaders. In fact, both sets of cheerleaders were performing at the same time—you just noticed them in sequence because you could only see one group at a time. If you could see 360 degrees around you all at once, everything would be happening at the same time and there would be no apparent sequencing of events.

On the Spirit Side, everything happens continuously and concurrently in one moment of time—the present. Souls can focus on whatever event or activity they desire and then change their focus to something else whenever they choose, but everything happens at the same time.

I have a lot of trouble getting my head around this concept. Everything around me and everything I do every day is affected by time, and it is difficult to comprehend a place where there is no past or future, only a present.

It is not important that you understand this now. You understood this concept before you incarnated, and you will understand this reality once again when you return to the Spirit Side. While you are on Earth, you must accept the fact that you have to live with the limitations of your human mind that restrict your ability to comprehend fully what I have told you about time on the Spirit Side.

Chapter Twelve

Soul Memories

It is very frustrating, Albert, to have to live with the limitations of my human mind, especially when you tell me I have so much more knowledge when I am on the Spirit Side. Can you tell me why I cannot access all my memories of the Spirit Side and previous lives?

If you remembered all your past lives, it would be a difficult burden for you to carry in your current life. You would remember all the bad things you had done in previous lives, as well as all the physical and emotional pain you had suffered at the hands of other people. These memories would be very distressful, and you would spend too much time trying to deal with your guilt for your past misdeeds and your anger or sadness for the hurtful actions of others. These memories would be distracting, and they would interfere with your ability to live your life according to your Life Plan.

Also, if you could recall the happiness and love you enjoyed on the Spirit Side before you were born, it would be more difficult for you to continue your journey as planned. Life on Earth is not easy because Earth is a difficult school. If you remembered how wonderful the Spirit Side was, and you knew you would return there after you died, it would be very tempting for you to hasten your return by taking your life. This would end your incarnation before you had a chance to encounter everything your Soul had proposed when it created your Life Plan.

Finally, any recollection of the details of your Life Plan would prejudice your adventure since you would know in advance what events were likely to happen and how you were supposed to react to them. This would be like high school teachers giving their students the questions and answers to final exams before the tests. There would be no point for the students to write the exam, and no one would need to study for it.

Are there any exceptions to this rule? Is it ever possible for these memories to come through to us as we live our lives?

Sometimes a few of these memories will leak through to a human mind, either directly or subconsciously. In these cases, the ability of a person to access such memories usually results from a concerted effort by the person's Spirit Guides to open channels of awareness to assist in advancing the individual's Life Plan agenda.

There are numerous examples of this. The most common one is the feeling of "déjà vu" that many people have had at one time or another. Often this occurs when they travel to a place for the first time and get a strange feeling that they have been there before because the surroundings seem familiar. In most of these cases, they are accessing a residual memory of a previous life when they lived in that city.

In a few cases, memories of a past life show through in a new life as flashes of musical or artistic talent, especially in child prodigies. Mozart began composing music when he was five, an age when most other children are playing with toys. Most likely, he was able to access memories of a previous life as a musician and composer, and thus he got a head start in his new incarnation. Often Souls who have dedicated their lives on Earth to a particular pursuit will reincarnate as a person who can continue this passion in another life. Sometimes young children will be able to describe the details of a place they have never visited before and/or understand a language they have never been exposed to in their current lives. These children are remembering places and events from a previous life.

On the negative side, past-life memories can trigger fears or phobias in humans. Maybe those individuals who have a strong fear of water might be accessing a residual memory of drowning in a previous life. Perhaps those terrified of heights may have died that way in another life. Occasionally, these residual memories of events from a past life result in physical anomalies in a person's current life. A person with a

medically inexplicable painful leg might be tapping into a memory of a previous life as a soldier during World War I when he died from a gunshot wound in his thigh.

I have often wondered about this when I look back on my life. One of my shortcomings has been a lack of patience. I feel very frustrated when things do not happen fast enough. Now I am thinking that maybe I am accessing residual memories of the Spirit Side where everything happens instantly through thought creation, so the process of creation on this world seems incredibly slow by comparison.

In your case, this does contribute to your impatience although it does not excuse you from trying to overcome this tendency so that you can appreciate the Earth you are living in now and learn from your journey. Remember, you chose to incarnate on Earth, and you knew the conditions you would be facing in your new life, so do not complain about the slow-motion events on your planet. You will be back on the Spirit Side soon enough where you will once again be able to enjoy the speed of *thought creation*. Until then, you will have to live your life with all of the limitations that you now endure.

You said that one of the reasons humans cannot access their pre-birth memories is that they might be tempted to take their own lives in order to hasten their return to the comfort and happiness of the Spirit Side. As you know, most societies abhor suicide, and many religions consider it a grave sin. Is suicide contrary to God's laws? Is it possible for a Soul to include suicide in its Life Plan?

Suicide, like everything else that happens on Earth, is not inherently wrong. God does not punish anyone for committing suicide just as He does not punish Souls for anything else they do in their lives.

Most societies regard suicide as the cowardly act of desperate individuals unwilling to persevere with the life that God created for them. Suicide is viewed as a sin because it is thought to thwart God's plans for these individuals. Historically, however, a few societies did not regard suicide as being universally bad. In Roman times, a disgraced citizen was expected to do the honorable thing and fall on his sword. In feudal Japan, samurai warriors who were about to be captured were expected to die with honor by committing seppuku, a ritualized form of suicide.

On the Spirit Side, suicide is discouraged when it used as an escape from the hardships and difficulties that people might face in their lives because these circumstances were likely something their Souls had wanted to endure when they created their Life Plans. In many of these cases, these individuals are blocking all positive messages from their Souls and Spirit Guides and refusing to accept that they have created their own reality. Quite often, they believe they are victims who have been treated harshly and unfairly and have no hope for a better future. Sometimes individuals commit suicide to hurt other people, such as spouses and/or children, as an act of revenge for their previous hurtful actions.

Even though people who commit suicide are not punished for doing so, in most cases it results in partially wasted lives because they missed some of the important challenges they had hoped to experience. Once back on the Spirit Side, these Souls will realize they need to return to Earth in another life to try again. On rare occasions, it is possible for a Soul to include suicide as an exit point in its Life Plan.

If a person is contemplating a suicide that is not a Life Plan exit point, how will the Spirit Guides react?

They will try to persuade the person to hang in there, usually by coaching via embedded messages during the individual's sleep and dreaming states.

You have mentioned several times now that we often receive messages from the Spirit Side when we sleep. Can you expand on this?

Sleep is a "time out" for the body and mind, as well as the Soul. As you have figured out by now, life on Earth is not easy; it is full of discomfort and pain. On the human level, sleep allows the body to be at rest to allow for growth and rejuvenation. For the mind, it is a period when it can shut down and block out the constant barrage of physical and emotional data it receives while awake, thus providing a respite from the turmoil caused by analyzing and reacting to this information.

Most importantly, sleep allows a Soul to escape from its human form and journey to the Spirit Side. Since a Soul experiences everything its human experiences in its life, it needs a periodic break from this action to give it the opportunity to reflect on the events of the day.

What does a Soul do when it leaves its human during sleep?

It goes to the Spirit Side to meet with its Spirit Guides and other Souls in its spirit group. It will discuss the recent events in its life and review the upcoming schedule in its Life Plan. Its Spirit Guides will give it advice and loving encouragement.

It is similar to a football game on your planet. At half time, the players leave the field to go into the locker room where they can relax and rest their tired bodies. Their coaches will review the plays of the first half and offer suggestions on how they might have avoided their mistakes. They will give the team a pep talk in order to send them back onto the playing field with a positive attitude.

Similarly, when people are asleep, their Souls will listen to the advice of their Spirit Guides and reflect on what has happened so far in their lives. Quite often their Souls will adjust their Life Plans based on this guidance.

I can understand why a Soul needs an escape from life on this planet. Is this why many people have a difficult time getting up in the morning and why they feel sleepy at bedtime?

Since everything is so pleasant on the Spirit Side, a Soul is often reluctant to return to its body in the morning for another day on Earth, and it is eager to return to the Spirit Side each night, which influences the actions and tendencies of the human it occupies.

I have noticed in my life that I seem to need less sleep now than when I was younger, and I do not have to struggle to get up in the morning as I did years ago. Why does this happen?

It's part of your Soul's progression with your incarnation. When you were born and your Soul first entered your body, the whole ordeal was unpleasant and challenging. Remember that your Soul came from the Spirit Side and life on your world is quite harsh in contrast. At this early stage of your life, your Soul needed more time out of your body than it does now, and that is why you spent more time sleeping when you were a baby. As you grew older, your Soul became more accustomed to being in your body and putting up with the hardships, and now it has less need to escape.

Does my Soul leave my body only during my regular nightly sleep, or does it also leave during a nap?

Your Soul also leaves your body during a nap, even if it is a very short nap.

One other aspect of sleep has occurred to me. Often when people are facing a tough choice, such as whether to buy a new car or accept a job offer, they will put off making the decision

*for a day so they can "sleep on it." I have often found it easier
to make a tough decision after a good night's sleep.*

**This happens quite often. Your mind has an intuitive
sense that it should get guidance on these matters
from your Spirit Guides, and a period of sleep will
give your Soul the opportunity to consult with your
Spirit Guides and then communicate the answer to
you. So when you are feeling distressed or you are
struggling to make a decision, you will be able to cope
with it better after a period of sleep.**

Chapter Thirteen

The Law of Attraction

You have been very good at answering all my questions so far, Albert, and I wonder if I can bother you for your opinion about a belief that has become popular in the past few years—the Law of Attraction. There have been several best-selling books that have touted this theory, and many people believe it works. The main thesis of this "law" is that "like attracts like," and thoughts and intentions are powerful creators in the universe. If a person has positive thoughts and says, "I am going to acquire a lot of money," or "my future will be full of wealth and success," then the universe will bestow money and success on this person.

What is your view on the Law of Attraction?

It is true that thoughts are the starting point for the creation of all things in the universe although the proponents of the Law of Attraction often exaggerate the power and effectiveness of thoughts on the Earth plane. On the Spirit Side, thoughts are very powerful, and the things they create happen instantly through

165

thought creation. Since there are no shortages of anything on the Spirit Side, there are never any conflicting or competing thoughts on the Spirit Side.

The Earth plane, however, is very different. Thoughts on Earth are still creative, but they are not as powerful as thoughts on the Spirit Side. It takes longer for their creations to materialize. This is because the Earth plane has a lower vibration rate and a denser mass than the Spirit Side, and things happen at a slower pace. As I mentioned before, this slow-motion *thought creation* was designed to provide an interval of linear time between the start of an action and its completion, so humans (and their Souls) would have an opportunity to understand the effects of their thoughts and actions on other people.

In my previous example of the apple, your initial thought that you would like to eat an apple leads to a series of events, such as driving to the store, buying an apple, and returning home, that fulfills your desire. You could fulfill your wish even faster if you happened to have an apple in your cupboard. Unlike on the Spirit Side, however, an apple would not appear instantly in your hand as soon as you expressed your desire to have one.

This creative process does not always work for every person. If you are lost in the middle of the Sahara Desert, and you desire an apple, you will not be able to drive to the supermarket to get one. It might take several weeks before you find a city that has apples for sale, or you might perish from thirst before you find one. If the object of your desire is in short supply (which often is the case), it might take a long time before you have one in hand, if at all. On the Spirit Side, if all Souls want an apple at the same time, they can all have one instantly with *thought creation*.

Since Earth does not have an unlimited supply of all the material goods that humans need or want, many of their desires are not fulfilled. On the other hand, if a person seeks happiness, this can be achieved even if everyone else wants the same thing since happiness is a state of mind that is not dependent on how much stuff a person has.

The power of thought on Earth is magnified in direct proportion to the number of people who desire the same result. The simultaneous thoughts of a hundred people desiring exactly the same thing will have a greater influence than the desire of only one person. Even if is not organized, group thought affects things on a regular basis.

Are you saying the Law of Attraction does not always work because of the conflicting desires of humans for the limited supply of material goods available to them?

That is one reason. When more than one person wants something that is unique or in short supply, some individuals will not have their wishes fulfilled due to the physical limitations of the Earth plane. The other reason it does not always work is that it focuses on the earthly desires of the mind, such as having more money, a better job, or a bigger house. Often the fulfillment of such desires is contrary to what the Soul wanted to experience when it planned its life, and there is a basic conflict between the mind and the Soul. For example, if a person wants to have a million dollars, the Soul of this individual might be against this happening because doing so would cause the person to quit working and travel around the world for a year, thereby missing the opportunity to compete for a big career promotion—an event the Soul had mapped out in its Life Plan. When this tug-of-war happens, a person's Soul will send strong mental messages to cancel or change the unwanted desire, which often causes the mind subconsciously to follow the wishes of the Soul.

If I do not always get what I wish for, is it possible my Soul does not want my wish fulfilled because it would be contrary to my Life Plan, and it is working actively behind the scenes to thwart my desires?

This is true in many cases. You should always listen to your Soul and not just focus on the desires of your mind. You will know you are on the right track if it feels good in your heart.

Chapter Fourteen

The Book of Albert

About a year after my first meeting with Albert, I retired from my law practice. I continued my conversations with Albert as I struggled to write my book. I would often sit on our patio with my laptop on my knees although I was frequently distracted by the golfers going by on the ninth fairway. Even though golfing seemed like a better alternative, I knew I had to keep plugging away on this book, or I would never finish it. I often wondered how I got myself into this project since I had hoped retirement would allow me to spend most of my days golfing, hiking, kayaking, or lounging in the sun and reading a good book. Instead, I had to spend a good chunk of every day writing about my conversations with Albert. With my luck, I knew I could die before I had a chance to enjoy my golden years. And if nobody read my book, what would I have to show for all my effort? I knew it was time once again to check in with Albert.

I am a bit concerned, Albert, about writing a book about our conversations as you have suggested. Almost all of the things you have told me are "way out there," and many people will think I have lost my mind or that I am suffering from dementia.

Others will be angry that I have tried to undermine the foundations of their religious beliefs. A few of my friends and relatives will shun me. Writing this book will change my life—everything will be different.

Your predictions might happen although there will be fewer people with negative reactions to your book than you now expect. While some people will shun you, many will give you credit for taking the stand you will take in your book even if they do not agree with you. However, a large group of readers will embrace your book, and their lives will be enriched with the wisdom gained from the revelations we have passed on to you. We have chosen you to be our messenger on Earth to propagate our truths to the multitudes. What each person does in response to your book is entirely up to that individual who always has the right to exercise free will.

In any event, if you would rather not write the book because of the negative reactions you expect to receive, I will understand, and we will find another human to convey our message.

I will not turn back now. I value the conversations we have had, Albert, and I am honored you have chosen me to be your messenger. Where do we go from here?

Sit at your keyboard and start writing. The words will flow naturally with a little help from your friends here on the Spirit Side. Several of the spirits who are helping you have written extensively during their own

incarnations, and you can learn much from them. You only have to sit quietly, listen carefully, and follow your heart.

Do not be overly concerned about what other people might think about you. If you lose all of your friends because of your book, we can always hang pork chops around your neck so the dogs will play with you.

Has anyone ever told you to go to hell?

Many times. But I am happy to report that I have never been there—and I am not going back again.

Chapter Fifteen

Dancing on a Stamp

We have been having these conversations off and on for a couple of years now, Albert, and you have been very good about answering all my questions. I have learned a lot from you, and I am happy to write a book about our conversations as you have requested. Before I finalize my book, do you have any other words of wisdom for me?

First and foremost, always remember that you are an eternal Soul. You will exist forever and, no matter what you do or say during your life, you will always return to the peace and happiness of the Spirit Side. It was your decision to incarnate on Earth, and you chose the significant events of your life before you were born. When your physical body dies, you will leave it behind like an empty shell, and you will cross over to the Spirit Side where you will be reunited with everyone you have ever loved. No one will judge or punish you for anything you did in this life, and you will retain your memories and personality from all your previous lives. All your experiences will add to

your wisdom and increase your awareness of yourself as Soul who is part of God, the Creator.

These things are not easy to remember as you struggle with the day-to-day demands of your life. I have had many of my own incarnations on your planet, and I know it is difficult to remember who you really are in the midst of dealing with the events in your life that are often challenging and overwhelming. You must strive to remember these truths every day as they will lighten the burdens of your life and motivate you to treat other people and creatures with greater love and compassion.

You should be mindful of the words of Shakespeare when he said, "All the world's a stage." He was right. The Earth is like a stage, and all humans are acting in a grand play. Your life is like being a male lead in a Broadway play; the actor plays the role scripted for him by the playwright just like you, as an incarnated human, follow the script you prepared for yourself in your Life Plan. The actor does not have any trepidation about playing a part that requires him to suffer injuries or hardships since he knows it is only a play, and when he leaves the theatre after each performance, he will be back in reality. The actor strives to do his best to play the part, but he knows that he may flub his lines or miss cues. No matter how many mistakes he makes on stage, he knows it is not the end of the world, and he can always try to do better in his next performance. He does not feel any hatred or animosity toward the other actors who were cruel to him in the play; he understands that they were following the script, and the play is not "real life" anyway.

Likewise, you should try to remember that all other people are following their scripts, and nothing that occurs on Earth is "for keeps." No matter what happens to you, whether it is good fortune or bad luck, it does not last, and you will not take it with you. You will return to the Spirit Side when you die where you will enjoy only love and happiness, regardless of how you performed during your life.

When you interact with other people in your life, try to remember they are Souls just like you, who are struggling to cope with their lives without the benefit of knowing where they came from or where they will go after they die. They are Souls playing their parts in that great theater called Earth, except they do not even know they are in a play. Do not judge other people for their actions since you do not know where they have been or where they are going.

Try to understand that people who have inflicted physical or emotional pain on you or your family are not inherently bad and deserving of retribution. They may have agreed to play this part in your "play" at your request, or perhaps they are new Souls to the Earth plane who are not very adept at controlling their negative emotions. Remember that you have lived on Earth many times before this life, and you, too, have been guilty of mean and cruel deeds. Resist

175

the urge to strike back at those who harm you because you are all connected to each other and to God; whatever you do to others, you also do to yourself. Always forgive others for their transgressions and hold no grudges since one day you will all be back on the Spirit Side where the events of this life will only be distant memories, and you will once again share unconditional love for them and all other Souls.

If you notice a bug on the sidewalk as you walk down the street, do not step on it; let it live its life according to its own agenda and recognize that it is one of God's creations. Do not abuse the other creatures living on your planet; treat them all with dignity and respect and understand that they all have their own place in the universe.

As you make your way through life, try to see the face of God in the eyes of a homeless man when you drop money in his hat, in the smile of a little boy when a puppy licks his face, and in the tears of joy of a young mother when she cradles her newborn for the first time. Rejoice at the splendor of the sun sinking slowly into the ocean, the brilliance of a full moon on a cloudless night, and the majesty of a snow-capped mountain peak in the early morning sunlight. Marvel at the beauty of a cherry tree in full bloom and the grandeur of an ancient redwood tree. Feel the joy in your heart as you watch a hummingbird sucking nectar from the honeysuckle or a newborn fawn taking its first steps. Feel the presence of God in all the people around you and in all the creatures, plants, rocks, and oceans that exist on your planet. Try to acknowledge every day of your life that all things on Earth, whether animate or inanimate, are connected to everything else that exists in the universe. All form part of the totality that is God.

Heed the advice of Dr. James Martin Peebles when he said you should have "loving allowance for all things to be in their own time and place, beginning with yourself." Understand that you must first love and forgive yourself before you can truly love and forgive others.

Above all, you need to lighten up and enjoy the ride. Do not take everything so seriously. You cannot go wrong or become lost. Regardless of what you do in this life, you will end up back on the Spirit Side to live another day. Look at your life as an exciting adventure and relish the experience. Keep a smile on your face and laugh freely every chance you get because laughter will bring joy to your life and spread cheer to everyone around you.

You are in the middle of a big, beautiful ballroom with hardwood floors that gleam brightly from the sunlight streaming in through the stained-glass windows. The band is playing irresistible dance music that has all on their feet in a dance of joy. Yet all too often you have remained on one spot, dancing as though you are wearing leg irons and a strait jacket.

Break free of your shackles. Quit dancing on a stamp. Let yourself swirl around the whole ballroom. Feel the rhythm of the music as it resonates through your body. Let your feet slide, your arms pump, and your body sway to the music. You came here to experience this ballroom, so get to know it. Dance like no one is watching, and let your heart sing with the joy of being alive. When the music stops, you will leave this ballroom to find your next adventure. Enjoy your journey.

About the Author

Garnet Schulhauser practiced corporate law with two large law firms in Calgary, Canada for 34 years before retiring to Vancouver Island in 2008, where he now lives with his wife, Cathy, and little dog, Abby. He grew up on a small farm in Saskatchewan and attended law school in Saskatoon before moving to Calgary to begin his legal career. Although he did not begin writing until after retiring from his legal practice, he now pursues his new career with a passion. In his spare time, he enjoys golfing, kayaking, and long hikes in the forest with his dog. He takes great delight in family gatherings with his two sons, Blake (and his wife, Lauren) and Colin, and looks forward to the arrival of grandchildren some day.

Garnet's life changed dramatically one day in 2007 when he was confronted on the street by a homeless man named Albert. Over the next few years he had a series of conversations with Albert (who was actually a wise spirit guide in disguise) who disclosed startling new truths about life, death, the afterlife, and God. Albert answered all of life's big questions about who we are, our purpose for being on Earth, and what happens to us after we die. Albert's revelations were inspiring, uplifting, and comforting, and flew in the face of almost everything that Christian holy men had been preaching for centuries. He wrote *Dancing on a Stamp* at Albert's request so that these revelations would be available to everyone.

Other Books Published
by
Ozark Mountain Publishing, Inc.

Conversations with Nostradamus, Volume I, II, III..............by Dolores Cannon
Jesus and the Essenes..by Dolores Cannon
They Walked with Jesus..by Dolores Cannon
Between Death and Life.. by Dolores Cannon
A Soul Remembers Hiroshima...by Dolores Cannon
Keepers of the Garden..by Dolores Cannon
The Legend of Starcrash..by Dolores Cannon
The Custodians...by Dolores Cannon
The Convoluted Universe - Book One, Two, Three, Four......by Dolores Cannon
Five Lives Remembered ....by Dolores Cannon
The Three Waves of Volunteers and the New Earth .... by Dolores Cannon
I Have Lived Before...by Sture Lönnerstrand
The Forgotten Woman...by Arun & Sunanda Gandhi
Luck Doesn't Happen by Chance...................................by Claire Doyle Beland
Mankind - Child of the Stars.............................by Max H. Flindt & Otto Binder
Past Life Memories As A Confederate Soldier.......................by James H. Kent
Holiday in Heaven...by Aron Abrahamsen
Out of the Archives .... by Aron & Doris Abrahamsen
Is Jehovah An E.T.?..by Dorothy Leon
The Essenes - Children of the Light...............by Stuart Wilson & Joanna Prentis
Power of the Magdalene................................by Stuart Wilson & Joanna Prentis
Beyond Limitations ....by Stuart Wilson & Joanna Prentis
Atlantis and the New Consciousness .... by Stuart Wilson & Joanna Prentis
Rebirth of the Oracle................................by Justine Alessi & M. E. McMillan
Reincarnation: The View from Eternity......by O.T. Bonnett, M.D. & Greg Satre
The Divinity Factor..by Donald L. Hicks
What I Learned After Medical School ....by O.T. Bonnett, M.D.
Why Healing Happens...by O.T. Bonnett, M.D.
A Journey Into Being...by Christine Ramos, RN
Discover The Universe Within You..by Mary Letorney
Worlds Beyond Death..by Rev. Grant H. Pealer
A Funny Thing Happened on the Way to Heaven .... by Rev. Grant H. Pealer
Let's Get Natural With Herbs..by Debra Rayburn
The Enchanted Garden..by Jodi Felice
My Teachers Wear Fur Coats.......................by Susan Mack & Natalia Krawetz
Seeing True..by Ronald Chapman
Elder Gods of Antiquity...by M. Don Schorn
Legacy of the Elder Gods...by M. Don Schorn
Gardens of the Elder Gods .... by M. Don Schorn
Reincarnation...Stepping Stones of Life ....by M. Don Schorn

Continue for more books by Ozark Mountain Publishing, Inc.

For more information about any of the above titles, soon to be released titles, or
other items in our catalog, write or visit our website:

OZARK
MOUNTAIN
PUBLISHING

PO Box 754
Huntsville, AR 72740
www.ozarkmt.com
1-800-935-0045/479-738-2348
Wholesale Inquiries Welcome